HUMAN CAPITAL MANAGEMENT

HUMAN CAPITAL MANAGEMENT

ACHIEVING ADDED VALUE THROUGH PEOPLE

Angela Baron & Michael Armstrong

KOGAN PAGE

London and Philadelphia

First published in Great Britain and the United States in 2007 by Kogan Page Limited

120 Pentonville Road
London N1 9JN
United Kingdom
www.kogan-page.co.uk

525 South 4th Street, #241
Philadelphia PA 19147
USA

© Angela Baron and Michael Armstrong, 2007

ISBN-10   0 7494 4938 1
ISBN-13   978 0 7494 4938 4

British Library Cataloguing-in-Publication Data

A CIP record for this book is available from the British Library.

Library of Congress Cataloging-in-Publication Data

Armstrong, Michael, 1928–
    Human capital management : achieving added value through people / Michael Armstrong and Angela Baron.
        p. cm.
    Includes bibliographical references and index.
    ISBN-13: 978–0–7494–4938–4
    ISBN-10: 0–7494–4938–1
    1. Personnel management. 2. Human capital. I. Baron, Angela. II. Title.
    HF5549.A89776 2007
    658.3'01—dc22

                                                                              2006039736

Typeset by JS Typesetting Ltd, Porthcawl, Mid Glamorgan
Printed and bound in Great Britain by MPG Books Ltd, Bodmin, Cornwall

Contents

Establishing the link between HR practice and business
performance 154; Information on intangible value for
the investment community 157; Convincing senior
management 157; Enlisting the interest and involvement
of line management 158; Convincing HR specialists 160;
Staged development of HCM 160; Developing the HCM
skills of HR specialists 162; The meaning of added value 163;
What is meant by regarding people as assets 164; Selecting
the measures 165; Analysing and evaluating the data 166;
The future of external reporting 166; Conclusions 169

Foreword

So what is human capital? The term has probably set off more emotions in the HR world than any other. On the one hand its proponents hail it as a revolutionary way of managing people, treating them as assets rather than costs. On the other, detractors see is as just another HR fad. Some practitioners are embracing the challenge with enthusiasm while others feel daunted and confused by the array of tools and techniques and the need to have at least a passing acquaintance with numbers. Even the very phrase 'human capital' leads to heated debate with on the one side those who believe it dehumanizes the people element of the enterprise to the other who believe it finally puts people on the right side of the balance sheet.

Whether we like it or love it the term 'human capital' is here to stay and is now accepted as a common definition of the all important people element of intangible value. Intangible value is constantly increasing in importance as the very existence of most of our organizations depends on our ability to innovate, to capture the support of customers, to establish our brand and to respond to an ever-changing marketplace. All of this depends on people and getting the best from people depends on understanding what motivates them to perform, to give outstanding service to customers, to run that extra mile when it counts. Without this information, managers have to make decisions largely in ignorance of the impact these decisions might have on the performance of people.

What this book tries to do is demystify some of the loftier claims for human capital management and demonstrate that any practitioner in any organization can get better at providing the information that will help them understand just what it is that their people contribute. This in turn will improve management decision making and help them move towards developing strategic measures to help identify the drivers of success in their business.

Human capital management is a journey. Where you start will largely depend on the information available. Where you go will depend on what you do with that information and how you are able to grow and communicate it. The kind of practical guidance, tools and analysis of the literature contained in this book will help managers to build themselves a route map to continue that journey whatever their starting point.

The use of quality people data is the key to good human capital management. Analyse and link this data with business performance metrics (such as sales, customer service and financial performance) and you begin to get deep organizational insight into how effective your people strategy is and its impact on business performance and the bottom line.

Human capital is often represented as both a challenge and an opportunity. A challenge to identify relevant measures and provide meaningful information which can be acted on, and an opportunity to both evaluate and maximize the value of people.

Neil Roden
Group Director, Human Resources
The Royal Bank of Scotland Group

Acknowledgements

Books like this can never be completed without the support and involvement of a wide range of individuals. We are therefore very grateful to all those who encouraged us to write this book. However, our most grateful thanks must go to all the busy HR professionals who gave up their time to be interviewed and give their views, particularly the members of the Chartered Institute of Personnel and Development's (CIPD's) Human Capital Panel.

Introduction

Human capital management (HCM) was described by the Accounting for People Task Force (2003) as 'a strategic approach to people management that focuses on the issues that are critical to the organization's success'. It treats people management 'as a high-level strategic issue and seeks systematically to analyse, measure and evaluate how people policies and practices create value'. Scarborough and Elias (2002) noted that the most useful contribution of human capital to date is in defining the link between HR and business strategy. The Chartered Institute of Personnel and Development (CIPD, 2006a) expanded on this idea as follows: 'A human capital approach implies that a realistic business strategy must be informed by human capital data. In other words how can a business pursue a strategy that doesn't take account of the capacity of all the resources available, including the human ones?'

HCM is concerned with measurement (metrics) but there is more to it than that. As Duncan Brown, Assistant Director of the CIPD commented in 2006: 'Human capital management is not primarily about measurement. It is about creating and demonstrating the value that great people and great people management add to an organization.'

Donkin (2005) believes that the organizational strength of HCM lies in three areas: 'development and application of relevant measures, both quantitative and qualitative; gathering and interpreting results; utilising this information for strategic advantage'. He continues:

'Companies that concentrate management efforts on these areas will be best positioned to align their employment policies with strategic intent. Good human capital management, therefore, is all about learning, understanding, intervening and adjusting.'

The prime object of this book is to provide a practical guide to how HCM policies and practices can help to deliver added value through people while continuing to meet their aspirations and needs. It deals with the processes of measurement and reporting but focuses on the process of critical evaluation of both quantitative and qualitative data and the use of predictive analysis to determine the future outcomes of existing and proposed practices. To achieve this the book takes the following approach:

1. Part 1 describes the concepts of human capital and HCM and provides an overall description of how the process of HCM works.

2. Part 2 extends the broad analysis contained in Part 1 by examining the practice of HCM as a sequence of activities beginning with data collection and continuing with measurements and reporting. It distinguishes data from measures. Human capital data is the basic raw material; measures assemble and analyse that raw material so that information is generated and reports are presented that inform HCM decisions. This part also considers the various applications of HCM with regard to HR strategy formulation, talent management learning and development, knowledge management, performance management and reward management.

3. The book concludes in Part 3 with an examination of the role of HR in HCM, the HR skills required and the future of the concept.

The book also contains in an appendix a toolkit that organizations can use to develop their own HCM policies and practices.

Part 1

The essence of HCM

1

The concept of human capital

The concept of human capital is concerned with the added value people provide for organizations. It has been well said by Chatzkel (2004) that 'it is human capital that is the differentiator for organizations and the actual basis for competitive advantage'. Human capital theory, as stated by Ehrenberg and Smith (1997), 'conceptualizes workers as embodying a set of skills which can be "rented out" to employers. The knowledge and skills a worker has – which come from education and training, including the training that experience brings – generate a certain *stock* of productive capital.

Human capital is an important element of the intangible assets of an organization. The other intangible assets include copyright, customer relations, brands and company image. All these, but especially the know-how, imagination and creativity of employees, are as critical to business success as 'hard' assets. The significance of human assets explains why it is important to measure their value as a means of assessing how well they are used and of indicating what needs to be done to manage them even more effectively.

As described by Scarborough and Elias (2002): 'The concept of human capital is most usefully viewed as a bridging concept – that is, it defines the link between HR practices and business performance in terms of assets rather than business processes.' They point out that human capital is to a large extent 'non-standardised, tacit, dynamic, context dependent and embodied in people'. These characteristics make it difficult to evaluate human capital bearing in mind that the 'features of human capital that are so crucial to firm performance are the flexibility and creativity of individuals, their ability to develop skills over time and to respond in a motivated way to different contexts'. They also mention that: 'In human capital theory, reference is made to people and skills, whilst in theories of physical capital, reference is made to plant and equipment.'

There are many definitions of human capital but in this book it is treated as one of the three elements that make up intellectual capital, the others being social capital and organizational capital. This chapter examines the meaning and significance of each of these elements.

INTELLECTUAL CAPITAL

Intellectual capital defined

Intellectual capital consists of the stocks and flows of knowledge available to an organization. These can be regarded as intangible resources which, together with tangible resources (money and physical assets), comprise the market or total value of a business. Bontis (1996; 1998), defines intangible resources as the factors other than financial and physical assets that contribute to the value-generating processes of a firm and are under its control. As described by Edvinson and Malone (1997), these comprise the value of all relationships inside and outside the organization, including those with customers and suppliers. They also cover the values attached to such intangibles as goodwill, corporate image and brands.

The elements of intellectual capital

The three elements of intellectual capital are:

∎ *Human capital* – the knowledge, skills, abilities and capacity to develop and innovate possessed by people in an organization.

∎ *Social capital* – the structures, networks and procedures that enable those people to acquire and develop intellectual capital represented by the stocks and flows of knowledge derived from relationships within and outside the organization.

∎ *Organizational capital* – the institutionalized knowledge possessed by an organization that is stored in databases, manuals, etc

(Youndt, 2000). It is often called *structural capital* (Edvinson and Malone, 1997), but the term organizational capital is preferred by Youndt because, he argues, it conveys more clearly that this is the knowledge that the organization actually *owns.*

The significance of intellectual capital

This tripartite concept of intellectual capital indicates that, while it is individuals who generate, retain and use knowledge (human capital), this knowledge is enhanced by the interactions between them (social capital) to generate the institutionalized knowledge possessed by an organization (organizational capital).

As Chatzkel (2004) points out: 'The reality is that organizations are nothing more than an extension of human thought and action.' It is the knowledge, skills and abilities of individuals that create value, and the focus has to be on means of attracting, retaining, developing and maintaining the human capital they represent. This individual knowledge is retained and put to use through knowledge management processes as described in Chapter 9, but it is equally important to take into account social capital considerations, that is, the ways in which knowledge is developed through interactions between people. It is pointed out by Bontis *et al* (1999) that it is flows as well as stocks that matter. Intellectual capital develops and changes over time and a significant part is played in these processes by people acting together.

Organizational effectiveness also depends upon making good use of this knowledge, which needs to be developed, captured and exchanged (knowledge management) in order to create organizational capital. In doing so, it should be remembered that, as stated by Daft and Weick (1984), 'individuals come and go, but organizations preserve knowledge over time'. Or, as expressed more colourfully by Fitz-enj (2000), 'organizational capital (knowledge) stays behind when the employee leaves; human capital is the intellectual asset that goes home every night with the employee'.

HUMAN CAPITAL

Origin of the concept

The term human capital was originated by Schultz (1961), an economist who proved that the yield on human capital investment through education and training in the United States was larger than that based on investment in physical capital. Schultz elaborated his concept in 1981 as follows: 'Consider all human abilities to be either innate or acquired. Attributes... which are valuable and can be augmented by appropriate investment will be human capital... By investing in themselves, people can enlarge the choices available to them.'

However, the idea of investing in human capital was first developed by Adam Smith (1776), who argued in the *Wealth of Nations* that differences between the ways of working of individuals with different levels of education and training reflected differences in the returns necessary to defray the costs of acquiring those skills. The return on investment in skills can therefore be compared to the returns from investing in physical capital. But this comparison has its limitations. Firms own physical capital but not their workers, except in a slave society.

Economists such as Elliott (1991) developed the theory of human capital. He is concerned with human capital in terms of the *quality*, not quantity, of the labour supply. He describes the decision to acquire or develop skills as an investment decision that requires the outlay of resources now for returns in the future and emphasizes that a major part of the human stock of economies takes the form of human capital. He comments that:

> When investing in individuals, firms have fewer guarantees, than they do with machines, that they can secure the continuing use of their services. Individuals, unlike machines, can always decide to leave the firm, or they can decide to withdraw their labour, strike, go absent or work badly. Human capital theory proposes that individuals will invest in human capital if the private benefits exceed the costs they incur and that they will invest up to the point at which the marginal return equals the marginal cost.

Human capital defined

Human capital consists of the intangible resources that workers provide for their employers. It was defined by Bontis *et al* (1999) as follows:

> Human capital represents the human factor in the organization; the combined intelligence, skills and expertise that gives the organization its distinctive character. The human elements of the organization are those that are capable of learning, changing, innovating and providing the creative thrust which if properly motivated can ensure the long-term survival of the organization.

Human capital is not owned by the organization but secured through the employment relationship. People bring human capital to the organization although it is then developed by experience and training. Davenport (1999) comments that:

> People possess innate abilities, behaviours and personal energy and these elements make up the human capital they bring to their work. And it is they, not their employers, who own this capital and decide when, how and where they will contribute it. In other words, they can make choices. Work is a two-way exchange of value, not a one-way exploitation of an asset by its owner.

The point emphasized by Davenport, that workers as well as employers invest in human capital, is in accord with the economic theory of human capital as described above. As expressed by Ehrenberg and Smith (1994), human capital theory 'conceptualises workers as embodying a set of skills which can be "rented out" to employers'.

For the worker, the expected returns on human capital investments are a higher level of earnings, greater job satisfaction, better career prospects, and, at one time, but less so now, a belief that security in employment is assured. In today's conditions, however, investments by workers in developing transferable skills can be attractive as means of increasing employability. The costs of such investments, as spelt out by Elliott (1991) take a psychological, social and monetary form. Psychological costs are those borne by individuals, perhaps the less able, who may find learning difficult. Social costs take the form of foregone market opportunities (ie opportunity costs – the time spent devoted to investing in human capital could have been spent in other activities). Monetary costs include both direct financial outlays and foregone market opportunities. As suggested by Elliott, the decision to acquire skills is an investment decision. Individuals will invest in human capital if they believe that the benefits to them will exceed the costs they will incur. These benefits consist of the net addition to life-long earnings that result from selling skilled rather than unskilled labour.

For the employer, the returns on investment in human capital is expected to be improvements in performance, productivity, flexibility and the capacity to innovate which should result from enlarging the skill base and increasing levels of knowledge and competence. Schuller (2000) suggests that: 'The general message is persuasive: skills, knowledge and competences are key factors in determining whether organizations and nations will prosper.' And Lepak and Snell (1999) comment that: 'The value of human capital is inherently dependent upon its potential to contribute to the competitive advantage or core competencies of the firm.'

Human capital theory can be associated with the resource-based view of the firm as developed by Barney (1991). This proposes that sustainable competitive advantage is attained when the firm has a human resource pool that cannot be imitated or substituted by its rivals.

It can also be associated with what might be called the competency movement on the grounds that competencies, effectively used, build value in organizations. The assessment of competency levels in performance management processes can reveal trends in the development of a competent workforce and therefore the value of that workforce. Ulrich (1998) states that human capital consists of 'competence × commitment'.

Workers as assets

The added value that people can contribute to an organization is emphasized by human capital theory. It regards people as assets and stresses that investment by organizations in people will generate worthwhile returns. An influential contribution to an understanding of this aspect of the concept was made by Becker (1975). As noted by Scarborough and Elias (2002):

> This applies a concept of human capital that is similar to theories of physical capital. In human capital theory, reference is made to people and skills, whilst in theories of physical capital, reference is made to plant and equipment. A theory of human capital places emphasis on the way in which employee competencies create value for the organization in the same way that the ownership of physical capital (this might be something like an oil field or a factory building) contributes to the performance of the firm. Thus, applying human capital theory to view the worker as an asset has significant implications for management practice. It leads to the conclusion that firms need to redefine the costs associated with remuneration, training and development and career progression as investments that create value for the business. The theory therefore underpins the philosophy of human resource management (HRM) which, as developed in the 1980s, stated that employees should be treated as assets rather than costs.

But it is maintained by Davenport (1999) that the concept of regarding people as assets is limited, indeed questionable, because:

▌ workers should not be treated as passive assets to be bought, sold and replaced at the whim of their owners – increasingly, they actively control their own working lives;

▌ the notion that companies own human assets as they own machines is unacceptable in principle and inapplicable in practice; it short-changes people by placing them in the same category as plant and equipment;

▌ no system of 'human asset accounting' has succeeded in producing a convincing method of attaching financial values to human resources; in any case, this demeans the more intangible added value that can be delivered to organizations by people.

Investments by employers in training and developing people is a means of attracting and retaining human capital as well as getting better returns from those investments. However, employers need to remember that workers, especially knowledge workers, may regard themselves as free agents who can choose how and where they invest their talents, time and energy.

Important though human capital theory may be, interest in it should not divert attention from the other aspects of intellectual capital – social and organizational capital – that are concerned with developing and embedding the knowledge possessed by the human capital of an organization. Schuller (2000) contends that: 'The focus on human capital as an individual attribute may lead – arguably has already led – to a very unbalanced emphasis on the acquisition by individuals of skills and competences which ignores the way in which such knowledge is embedded in a complex web of social relationships.'

Measuring the value of human capital

'The value of human capital is inherently dependent upon its potential to contribute to the competitive advantage or core competence of the firm' (Lepak and Snell, 1999).

The recognized importance of achieving human capital advantage (Boxall, 1996) has led to an interest in the development of methods of measuring the value of that capital for the following reasons:

▌ Human capital constitutes a key element of the market worth of a company and its value should therefore be included in the accounts as an indication to investors or those contemplating a merger or acquisition of the total value of a business, including its intangible as well as its tangible assets.

▌ The process of identifying measures and collecting and analysing information relating to them will focus the attention of the organization on what needs to be done to find, keep, develop and make the best use of its human capital.

▌ Measurements of the value of human capital can provide the basis for resource-based HR strategies that are concerned with the development of the organization's core competencies.

▌ Measurements can be used to monitor progress in achieving strategic HR goals and generally to evaluate the effectiveness of HR practices.

The first, and to a certain extent the second, of these arguments were advanced in a pioneering study by Hermanson (1964). His views were popularized by Likert (1967), and in the 1960s and 1970s efforts were made to get the notion accepted by investors and businesses; to no avail. Members of the accountancy profession have generally dismissed the idea because they believe that the figures would almost certainly be based on crude assumptions and, as Schuller (2000) comments, they would involve numerical precision which would be 'wholly out of line with these assumptions'. An authoritative report by the OECD (1998) states that: 'Measures of human capital have been strongly guided by what is possible to measure, rather than by what is desirable to measure.' The Accounting Standards Board, which sets the rules for financial accounting in the UK has stated, as reported by Outram (1998), that: 'We don't think you can solve problems by incorporating them in the accounts.'

According to Sackmann *et al* (1989) human resource accounting (often referred to as human asset accounting) aims to 'quantify the economic value of people to the organization' in order to provide input for managerial and financial decisions. Bontis *et al* (1999) refer to three types of human resource accounting models:

▌ cost models, which consider the historical, acquisition, replacement or opportunity cost of human assets;

▌ HR value models, which combine non-monetary behavioural with monetary economic value models;

▌ monetary models, which calculate discounted estimates of future earnings.

In their basic form, as indicated by Bontis *et al*, human resource accounting models attempt to calculate the contributions that human assets make to firms by capitalizing pay expenditures. A discounted cash flow of total pay is included in the asset section of the balance sheet rather than classifying it as an expense.

The problem with human resource or asset accounting is that, as Bontis *et al* point out: 'All of the models suffer from subjectivity and uncertainty and lack reliability in that the measures cannot be audited with any assurance.' It is for this reason that the notion of human resource accounting is not generally accepted by accountants or financial analysts. It can also be argued that it is morally unacceptable to treat people as financial assets and, in any case, people are not 'owned' by the company.

But people in organizations do add value and there is a case for assessing this value to provide a basis for HR planning and for monitoring the effectiveness and impact of HR policies and practices. This approach involves the assessment of the value or contribution to business success of HR practices generally rather than only measuring the value of human capital. The aims are to measure how efficiently organizations are using their human capital and, in the words of Mayo (1999), to assess 'the value of future earnings opportunities'.

SOCIAL CAPITAL

The concept of social capital has been defined by Putnam (1996) as 'the features of social life – networks, norms and trust – that enable participants to act together more effectively to pursue shared objectives'. The World Bank (2000) offers the following definition on its website: 'Social capital refers to the institutions, relationships and norms that shape the quality and quantity of a society's social interactions… Social capital is not just the sum of the institutions which underpin a society – it is the glue that holds them together.'

The World Bank also notes that social capital can be perceived as a set of *horizontal associations* between people, consisting of social networks and associated norms that have an effect on community, productivity and well-being (website accessed 2000). This brings us closer to the meaning and significance of the concept of social capital as an element of intellectual capital. It should be remembered that it is individuals, not organizations, who own human capital. Therefore, as Youndt (2000) claims, since employees are free, within limits, to leave their firm, there is a significant risk that organizations may incur an intellectual capital loss 'unless individual knowledge is transferred, shared, transformed and institutionalised'.

Social capital can be regarded as knowledge tied up and developed by relationships among employees, partners, customers and suppliers. It is built by the exchange of such knowledge and this requires a collaborative organizational environment in which knowledge and information can flow freely (Bontis, 1996, and Coleman, 1990).

It is necessary to capture individual knowledge through knowledge management processes as described, but it is equally important to take into account social capital considerations, that is, the ways in which knowledge is developed through interaction between people. Flows as well as stocks matter. Intellectual capital develops and changes over time and a significant part is played in these processes by people acting together. Such an environment is more likely to exist in a 'boundary-less' organization where the emphasis is on lateral processes, teams and task forces that can leverage knowledge across the business. Social capital, as Schuller (2000) puts it, 'enables human capital to realise its potential'. And the research conducted by Kinnie *et al* (2006) established that social capital actually plays a much bigger role as an element of intellectual capital than has previously been envisaged.

ORGANIZATIONAL CAPITAL

Organizational or structural capital consists of the knowledge owned by the organization rather than by individual employees. It can be described as *embedded* or *institutionalized* knowledge that may be retained with the help of information technology on readily accessible and easily extended databases. It can include explicit knowledge that has been recorded on a database or in manuals and standard operating procedures, or tacit knowledge that has been captured, exchanged and, as far as possible, codified.

Any process or procedure in an organization is constructed from the knowledge of individuals. As Davenport and Prusak (1998) comment: 'In theory this embedded knowledge is independent of those who developed it – and therefore has some organizational stability – an individual expert can disappear without bringing the process to a halt or reducing the company's stock of embedded knowledge.'

Organizational capital is created by people (human capital) but is also the outcome of social capital interactions. It belongs to the firm and can be developed by knowledge management processes that aim to obtain and record explicit and tacit knowledge.

PRACTICAL IMPLICATIONS OF INTELLECTUAL CAPITAL THEORY

The practical implications of intellectual capital theory are examined below under three headings dealing with:

1. *Human capital* issues concerning the attraction, retention, development and reward of people in order to create and maintain a skilled, committed and well-motivated workforce.

2. *Social capital* considerations relating to the design and development of organizations that enhance the processes of developing, capturing and disseminating knowledge.

3. *Organizational capital* issues concerned with knowledge management.

Human capital theory and HR practices

Human capital theory focuses attention on resourcing, HR development, and reward strategies and practices.

Resourcing strategies

Resourcing strategies are concerned with matching human capital resources to the strategic and operational needs of the organization and ensuring the effective utilization of those resources. The strategies contribute to the formulation of business strategy by defining future human capital requirements, identifying opportunities to make better use of human capital, and pointing out how human capital constraints may affect the implementation of the business plan unless action is taken. These constraints could include skill shortages, problems in recruiting and retaining people, low productivity, high absenteeism, insufficient flexibility or an employee relations climate that inhibits cooperation and commitment.

Resourcing strategies will be based on HR planning processes that ensure that human capital needs are identified and plans made to satisfy them. 'Make or buy' decisions may have to be made. To a greater or lesser extent, organizations can concentrate on growing their own talent and promoting from within (a 'make' decision). But they may decide to buy in workers from elsewhere who already have the capabilities they need (a 'buy' decision). A policy choice needs to be made on the extent to which a 'make' or 'buy' approach is adopted.

They will also be concerned with talent management – ensuring that talented people are attracted, developed and retained in accordance with organizational needs.

HR development strategies

HR development strategies are business led in that they are initiated by the strategic plans of the organization and driven by the HR plans that define knowledge, skills and competency requirements. The strategies will address issues relating to the development of the capabilities of individuals and teams. They will also be concerned with encouraging organizational and individual learning. HR development strategies aim to attract and retain human capital as well as develop it. This is in accordance with the concept that workers are human capital investors; they will place their investable capital where it can earn the highest return. They want to develop their skills, potential and employability. Employees who undertake to do this and deliver their promises are more likely to get and to keep the sort of human capability they need. This applies to all categories of employees, not just knowledge workers.

Reward strategies

From a financial reward point of view, the implication of human capital theory is that investment in people adds to their value to the firm. Individuals expect a return on their own investment and firms have to recognize that the increased value of their employees should be rewarded. Human capital theory encourages the use of skill-based or competency-based pay as a method of reward. It also underpins the concept of individual market worth. This indicates that individuals have their own value in the marketplace which they acquire and increase through investments by their employer and themselves in gaining extra expertise and competence by means of training, development and experience. The market worth of individuals may be considerably higher than the market rate of their jobs, and if they are not rewarded accordingly they may market their talents elsewhere.

But non-financial reward considerations should also be taken into account. If workers are investing their human capital they want to obtain a return not only in the form of opportunities to grow and to achieve but also in terms of being valued by their employer. Organizations need therefore to consider how to recognize accomplishments through performance management processes and formal recognition schemes.

Practical implications of social capital theory

Youndt (2000) comments that there is a strong link between social capital and value creation. This link can be strengthened, as Galbraith (1973) noted, by the creation of lateral relations such as task forces and teams (ie social capital) which facilitate information flow between interdependent departments, thereby eliminating or reducing costly information flows up and down hierarchical channels.

With regard to organization design, this means developing organizations that function by means of horizontal processes cutting across functional boundaries in delayered structures. Ghoshal and Bartlett (1993) suggest that such an organization should be regarded as 'a portfolio of dynamic processes'. These processes will include networking and the use of interdisciplinary project teams as means of developing, sharing and disseminating knowledge.

Social capital theory indicates that issues relating to organizational behaviour as well as structural matters need to be addressed. This means establishing organizational development programmes concerned with process, not structure or systems; with the way things are done rather than what is done. Process refers to the ways in which people act and interact. It is about the roles they play on a continuing basis to develop, exchange and apply knowledge and to deal with events and situations involving other people.

Organizational development programmes can be based on action research (Lewin, 1947) survey feedback, and process consultation (Schein, 1969). They may incorporate team-building interventions and culture change programmes that aim to operationalize values relating to communication, participation, cooperation and trust.

Practical implications of organizational capital theory

Cannon (2000) asserts that 'The cutting edge of economic growth is knowledge.' Organizational or structural capital theory underpins the practice of knowledge management. Organizational capital is created by people (human capital) but is also the outcome of social capital interactions. It belongs to the firm and can be developed by knowledge management processes that aim to obtain and record explicit and tacit knowledge.

CONCLUSIONS

Human capital theory focuses attention on practical issues relating to employee resourcing, development and reward, measuring the value of people, evaluating HR processes, organizational learning and knowledge management. While it may appear to support the 'hard' HRM philosophy of treating employees as assets, it modifies what could be regarded as one of the less savoury aspects of HRM theory by emphasizing that these 'assets' are not owned by the business. In theory, people can invest in their own future and can choose how and where to make that investment. In practice, the extent to which they can do this may be restricted in many cases, but it is certainly something that knowledge workers can do, and this fact needs to be taken into account in formulating resourcing and HR development policies.

From an organizational perspective, human capital theory generates the following practical questions:

▌ What skills have we got?

▌ What skills de we need now and in the future?

▌ How are we going to attract, develop and retain these skills?

▌ How can we develop a culture and environment in which organizational and individual learning takes place that meets both our needs and the needs of our employees?

▌ How can we provide for both the explicit and tacit knowledge created in our organization to be captured, recorded and used effectively?

From the viewpoint of individuals, the theory emphasizes that they have the right to expect first, that they will obtain a proper return for the investment of their time and efforts in an organization in terms of the development of their skills and capabilities, and second, that they will be given opportunities to increase their employability, inside and outside the organization.

2

The concept of HCM

This chapter starts with a definition of HCM and its aims. Reference is made to the views of a number of recent commentators on this subject and the chapter continues with a discussion of the relationship between the concept and practice of HCM and that of HRM. The chapter concludes with an examination of the concepts of human capital advantage and resource-based strategy, both of which are closely related to the concept of HCM.

HCM DEFINED

HCM is concerned with obtaining, analysing and reporting on data that informs the direction of value adding strategic, investment and operational people management decisions at corporate level and at the level of frontline management. It is, as emphasized by Kearns (2006), ultimately about value.

HCM is concerned with *purposeful* measurement, not just measurement. The defining characteristic of HCM is the use of metrics to guide an approach to managing people that regards them as assets and emphasizes that competitive advantage is achieved by strategic investments in those assets through employee engagement and retention, talent management and learning and development programmes. HCM provides a bridge between HR and business strategy.

The Accounting for People Task Force Report (2003) stated that HCM involves the systematic analysis, measurement and evaluation of how people policies and practices create value. The report defined HCM as 'an approach to people management that treats it as a high level strategic issue rather than an operational matter "to be left to the HR people"'. The Task Force expressed the view that HCM 'has been under-exploited as a way of gaining competitive edge'. As John Sunderland, Task Force member and Executive Chairman of Cadbury Schweppes plc commented: 'An organization's success is the product of its people's competence. That link between people and performance should be made visible and available to all stakeholders.'

Nalbantian *et al* (2004) emphasize the purposeful measurement aspect of HCM. They define human capital as: 'The stock of accumulated knowledge, skills, experience, creativity and other relevant workforce attributes' and suggest that HCM involves 'putting into place the metrics to measure the value of these attributes and using that knowledge to effectively manage the organization'.

HCM is sometimes defined more broadly without the emphasis on measurement. Chatzkel (2004) states that: 'Human capital management is an integrated effort to manage and develop human capabilities to achieve significantly higher levels of performance.' And Kearns (2005a) describes HCM as: 'The total development of human potential expressed as organizational value'. He believes that 'HCM is about creating value through people' and that it is 'a people development philosophy, but the only development that means anything is that which is translated into value'.

AIMS OF HCM

The four fundamental objectives of HCM are to:

■ determine the impact of people on the business and their contribution to shareholder value;

■ demonstrate that HR practices produce value for money in terms, for example, of return on investment (ROI);

■ provide guidance on future HR and business strategies;

∎ provide diagnostic and predictive data that will inform strategies and practices designed to improve the effectiveness of people management in the organization.

The more specific aims of HCM are summarized in Figure 2.1.

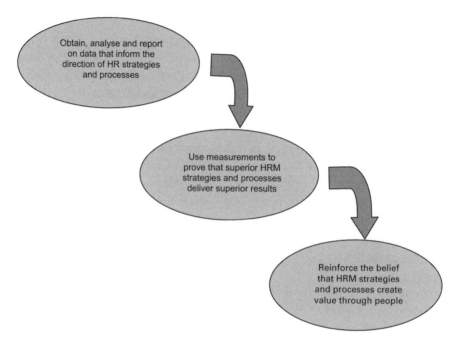

Figure 2.1 Aims of HCM

RATIONALE FOR HCM

HCM provides for evidence-based HRM. As Kearns (2006) stated: 'HCM can and should be in the interests of every stakeholder.' The DTI Accounting for People Task Force (2003) concluded that:

> Greater transparency on how value is created through effective people management policies and practices will benefit organizations and stakeholders. Managers, investors, workers, consumers and clients all have an interest in knowing that an organization is striving to adopt those features of HCM that are associated with high performance.

In the opinion of many of the FTSE 250 companies consulted by the Task Force and the CIPD, human capital evaluation and reporting is a 'must have' capability that is crucial to sustaining long-term performance. A number of the FTSE companies are concerned with making better quality information available on their human capital to both internal and external stakeholders and feel particularly under pressure from shareholders and customers to explain and justify the intangible value of their organizations. In knowledge-based industries in particular, obtaining, developing and retaining knowledge that can be embedded into goods and services is the key to success. As knowledge cannot be easily divorced from people, human capital information is particularly important in underpinning the processes that will enable organizations to manage their knowledge successfully.

Walters (2006) suggests that:

Effective HR processes need to be matched by an understanding of their impact on the cost-drivers of the business. Some of these linkages may be relatively straightforward and familiar (though perhaps still not fully evaluated or addressed) – for example, the business costs of labour turnover or absence. Other linkages may be less tangible or more difficult to quantify – for instance, the impact of employee engagement on factors such as productivity, service and quality. In all these cases, however, the adoption of a human capital approach, with appropriate processes for measurement and evaluation, is likely to help provide valuable insights into the dynamics of employee and business performance.

Matthewman (2006) believes that: 'HCM offers the opportunity for fact-based analysis, policy formulation and execution. In the past, too many HR projects were launched on instinct with little quantified success criteria or any calculation of the real return on investment (ROI).'

Managements are more likely to be persuaded by a business case if it is supported by data. As Mayo (2001) points out: 'managers are conditioned to working with numbers and nothing has a greater impact'.

HCM AND HRM

It is necessary to consider the difference, if any, between HCM and HRM. Is HCM an entirely separate activity? Or is it an aspect of HRM that highlights the significance of human capital measurement? In the opinion of Mayo (2001) the essential difference between HCM and HRM is that the former treats people as assets while the latter treats them as costs. Kearns (2005a) believes that in HCM 'people are value adders, not overheads' while in HRM 'people are [treated as] a significant cost and should be managed accordingly'.

The claim that in HRM employees are treated as costs is not supported by the descriptions of the *concept* of HRM produced by US writers such as Beer *et al* (1984). In one of the seminal texts on HRM they emphasized the need for 'a longer-term perspective in managing people and consideration of people as potential assets rather than merely a variable cost'. Fombrun *et al* (1984), in the other seminal text, quite explicitly presented workers as a key resource that managers use to achieve competitive advantage for their companies.

According to Kearns (2005a), in HRM 'the HR team is seen as a support service to the line' – HR is based around the function and the HR team performs 'a distinct and separate role from other functions.' Conversely, 'HCM is clearly seen and respected as an equal business partner at senior levels' and is 'holistic, organization-wide and systems-based' as well as being strategic and concerned with adding value. This assertion that HRM is simply what HR practitioners do in isolation from management is again not in accord with the generally accepted concept of HRM. In 1998, Legge defined the 'hard' model of HRM as a process emphasizing 'the close integration of human resource policies with business strategy which regards employees as a resource to be managed in the same rational way as any other resource being exploited for maximum return'. Guest (1987) believes that one of the key policy goals of HRM is strategic integration: 'The ability of the organization to integrate HRM issues into its strategic plans, ensure that the various aspects of HRM cohere, and provide for line managers to incorporate an HRM perspective into their decision-making'. He has stated (1991) that 'HRM is too important to be left to personnel managers.'

The concept of strategic HRM matches that of the broader definition of HCM quite well as is shown in the following definition of the main features of strategic HRM by Dyer and Holder (1998):

▌ *Organizational level* – because strategies involve decisions about key goals, major policies and the allocation of resources they tend to be formulated at the top.

▌ *Focus* – strategies are business-driven and focus on organizational effectiveness; thus in this perspective people are viewed primarily as resources to be managed toward the achievement of strategic business goals.

▌ *Framework* – strategies by their very nature provide unifying frameworks which are at once broad, contingency-based and integrative. They incorporate a full complement of HR goals and activities designed specifically to fit extant environments and to be mutually reinforcing or synergistic.

Both HRM in its proper sense and HCM as defined above treat people as assets. Although, as William Scott-Jackson, Director of the Centre for Applied HR Research at Oxford Brookes University argues (Oracle, 2005), 'You can't simply treat people as assets, because that depersonalises them and leads to the danger that that they are viewed in purely financial terms, which does little for all-important engagement.'

However, there is more to both HRM and HCM than simply regarding people as assets. Each of them also focuses on the importance of adopting an integrated and strategic approach to managing people, which is the concern of all the stakeholders in an organization not just the people management function.

So how does the concept of HCM reinforce or add to the concept of HRM? The answers to that question are that HCM:

▌ draws attention to the significance of what Kearns (2005a) calls 'management through measurement', the aim being to establish a clear line of sight between HR interventions and organizational success;

▌ provides guidance on what to measure, how to measure and how to report on the outcomes of measurement;

▌ underlines the importance of using the measurements to prove that superior people management is delivering superior results and to indicate the direction in which HR strategy needs to go;

▌ reinforces attention on the need to base HRM strategies and processes on the requirement to create value through people and thus further the achievement of organizational goals;

▌ defines the link between HRM and business strategy;

▌ strengthens the HRM belief that people are assets rather than costs;

▌ emphasizes the role of HR specialists as making a strategic contribution to business success.

The concept of HCM complements and strengthens the concept of HRM. It does not replace it. Both HCM and HRM can be regarded as vital components in the process of people management and both form the basis for achieving human capital advantage through a resource-based strategy.

THE CONCEPT OF HUMAN CAPITAL ADVANTAGE AND RESOURCE-BASED STRATEGY

The concept of human capital advantage as formulated by Boxall (1996) is based on the belief that sustainable competitive advantage is achieved when the firm has a HR pool that cannot be imitated or substituted by its rivals (Barney, 1991).

Unique talents among employees, including superior performance, productivity, flexibility, innovation and the ability to deliver high levels of personal customer service are ways in which people provide a critical ingredient in developing an organization's competitive position. People also provide the key to managing the pivotal interdependencies across functional activities and the important external relationships.

It can be argued that one of the clear benefits arising from competitive advantage based on the effective management of human capital is that such an advantage is hard to imitate. An organization's HR strategies, policies and practices are a unique blend of processes, procedures, personalities, styles, capabilities and organizational culture. One of the keys to competitive advantage is the ability to differentiate what the business supplies to its customers from what is supplied by its competitors. Such differentiation can be achieved by having HR strategies that ensure that the firm has higher quality people than its competitors, by developing and nurturing the unique intellectual capital possessed by the business and by focusing on organizational learning and knowledge management. This is the resource-based view of the firm and the rationale for a strategy based on it was produced by Grant (1991):

When the external environment is in a state of flux, the firm's own resources and capabilities may be a much more stable basis on which to define its identity. Hence, a definition of a business in terms of what it is capable of doing may offer a more durable basis for strategy than a definition based upon the needs (eg markets) that the business seeks to satisfy.

HCM and resource-based strategy have much in common. They both emphasize that a business strategy based on the acquisition, retention, motivation and development of high-quality people provides human capital and therefore competitive advantage.

CONCLUSIONS

The whole area of HCM presents both an opportunity and a challenge for the HR profession. It presents an opportunity to recognize people as an asset that contributes directly to organizational performance, and a challenge to develop the skills necessary to identify, analyse and communicate that contribution and ensure that it is recognized in business decision making. By developing better and more accurate information on human capital and communicating this both internally and externally, organizations will not only improve their business decision making but also enable various stakeholders to make more accurate assessments about the long-term future performance of the organization. There is evidence of a growing demand, from the investment community in particular, for better information to explain intangible value. Many organizations are beginning to understand that, in an increasingly knowledge-intensive environment, the key to good management lies in understanding the levers that can be manipulated to change employee behaviour and develop commitment and engagement. This, in turn, encourages individuals to deliver discretionary behaviour or willingly share their knowledge and skills to achieve organizational goals.

Systematically collected and analysed human capital data can really help managers to begin to understand factors that will have a direct impact on the people they manage. It can also help executives to understand and identify areas where there may have be issues regarding the effective management of staff and to design management development programmes to address these.

3

The process of HCM

The aim of this chapter is to provide an overview of the process of HCM which, as shown in Figure 3.1, is a journey in which the key stages are measurement, reporting, drawing conclusions from the data and action.

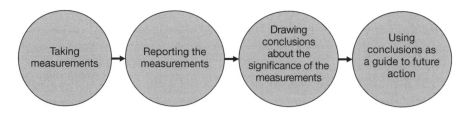

Figure 3.1   The process of HCM

The chapter starts with an assessment of the drivers of HCM and continues with a description of the human capital journey. The processes of measurement and reporting are then examined in more detail and the chapter ends with discussions on drawing conclusions and introducing HCM.

HCM DRIVERS

The question of what drives HCM needs to be answered before looking at the processes involved. The key drivers are:

▌ the need to achieve the strategic goals of the organization;

▌ the recognition that these goals can only be attained by the effective use of resources and that the key resource is people, whose knowledge, skills and abilities create value and produce human capital and therefore competitive advantage;

▌ an appreciation of the importance of understanding the factors that will create value through people;

▌ the realization that to understand and apply these factors it is necessary to measure and assess the actual or potential impact of HR processes and to base HR and business strategy on the outcomes of these measurements;

▌ the need to ensure that HR processes provide value for money.

The focus of HCM is illustrated in Figure 3.2.

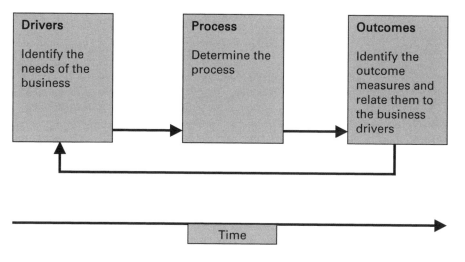

Figure 3.2 Human capital focus

THE HCM JOURNEY

The drivers influence how the process is used to generate particular outcomes and this means as our research has shown, that approaches will differ between organizations depending on their planned outcomes. So, for example, when the driver is internal to HR and about demonstrating value for money, the approach is very different to when it's about determining the impact of people on the business and the contribution to shareholder value.

Moreover, HCM is a dynamic and evolutionary process, as shown in Figure 3.3, which describes how the human capital journey produced by the drivers develops over time as organizations generate new needs and drivers.

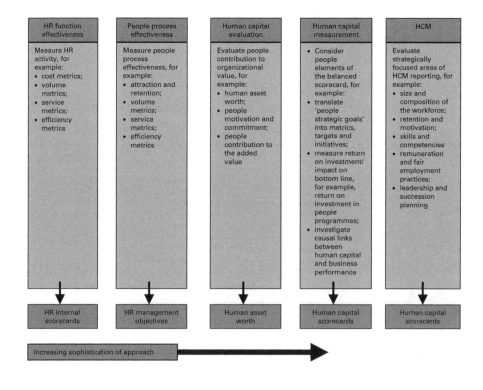

Source: CIPD (2004) *Human Capital Reporting: An internal perspective*, CIPD

Figure 3.3   The human capital pathway

It is important to emphasize the notion of HCM as a journey. It is not an all or nothing affair. It does not have to depend on a state of the art HR database or the possession of advanced expertise in statistical analysis. It is not all that difficult to record and report on basic data and, although some degree of analytical ability is required, it is to be hoped, nay expected, that any self-respecting HR professional will have that skill. At the beginning of the journey an organization may do no more than collect basic HR data on, for instance, employee turnover and absence. But anyone who goes a little bit further and analyses that data in order to draw conclusions on trends and causation leading to proposals on the action required that are supported by that analysis, is into HCM. Not in a big way perhaps, but it is a beginning. At the other end of the scale there are the highly sophisticated approaches to HCM operated by such organizations as the Nationwide Building Society and the Royal Bank of Scotland. This might be the ultimate destination of HCM but it can be approached on a step-by-step basis.

HUMAN CAPITAL MEASUREMENT

As Becker *et al* (2001) emphasize: 'The most potent action HR managers can take to ensure their strategic contribution is to develop a measurement system that convincingly showcases HR's impact on business performance.' They must 'understand how the firm creates value and how to measure the value creation process'. This means getting involved in human capital measurement as defined and described below bearing in mind that, as pointed out by Scarborough and Elias (2002) that the process of measurement can be just as important as the measurements themselves.

Definition

Human capital measurement has been defined by IDS (2004) as being 'about finding links, correlations and, ideally, causation, between different sets of (HR) data, using statistical techniques'. The CIPD (2004) emphasizes that it deals with the analysis of 'the actual experience of employees, rather than stated HR programmes and policies'.

Human capital measurement is based on human capital data comprising the numbers or quantities that describe human resources in an organization, represent particular aspects of the behaviour of people, or indicate the scale of different people management activities.

For example, the data may refer to demographic figures on the size and composition of the workforce, or the numbers of leavers, or absence figures, or the amount of training that has been carried out, or the number of vacancies that have been filled.

Human capital data can be necessary in itself for record keeping and to comply with various legal and regulatory requirements such as to ensure recruitment practices are not discriminatory or to comply with health and safety legislation. However, the data that is collected for these purposes is not always sufficient to inform on human capital. It can provide a useful starting point but needs to be considered in the light of what organizations need to know to understand their human capital and how it can be manipulated and analysed in order to provide this.

Data, therefore, needs to be distinguished from measures, as considered in the next chapter. Data is raw material; measures assemble and analyse that raw material so that conclusions can be reached on its value and significance.

Thus data may be available on the number of people leaving an organization over a certain period, but this will be interpreted as a measure of employee turnover – the number leaving as a percentage of the number employed. Data comes first, but establishing the need for a certain measure or metric may indicate what data is required to enable the measurement to take place. A metric is simply another word for a measure, although it has the connotation of being somehow more sophisticated.

Data as analysed and interpreted through measures provide *information* on human capital in order to provide the basis for evaluation, planning and action. In turn, the measures an organization uses to provide the information it needs on human capital may have implications not only for the type of data it collects but also for how this data is collected. Many organizations rely on data from computerized HR information systems that were designed for very different purposes. As a result they are experiencing difficulty with interpreting the data and ensuring that it is comparable with data collected by other means.

The next part of this book (Part 2) starts with Chapter 4, which explores the meaning and significance of human capital data. This provides the lead in to Chapter 5, which carries on with a description of how that data is turned into measures or, conversely, how the need for measures establishes the need for data. In turn, this leads to Chapter 6, which examines how the information provided by the data and measures is converted into reports as the basis for greater understanding and action.

The need for human capital measurement

There is an overwhelming case for evolving methods of valuing human capital as an aid to decision making. This may mean identifying the key people management drivers and modelling the effect of varying them. The issue is to develop a framework within which reliable information can be collected and analysed such as added value per employee, productivity and measures of employee behaviour (attrition and absenteeism rates, the frequency/severity rate of accidents, and cost savings resulting from suggestion schemes).

Becker *et al* (2001) refer to the need to develop a 'high-performance perspective' in which HR and other executives view HR as a system embedded within the larger system of an organization's strategy implementation. They state that: 'The firm manages and measures the relationship between these two systems and firm performance.' A high-performance work system is a crucial part of this approach in that it:

▌ links the firm's selection and promotion decisions to validated competency models;

▌ develops strategies that provide timely and effective support for the skills demanded by the firm's strategy implementation;

▌ enacts compensation and performance management policies that attract, retain and motivate high-performance employees.

Reasons for the interest in measurement

Human capital is a vital intangible asset in an organization that is as critical to business success as 'hard' assets', if not more so. The recognized importance of achieving human capital advantage has led to an interest in the development of methods of measuring the value of this intangible asset for the following reasons:

▌ Human capital constitutes a key element of the market worth of a company. A research study conducted in 2003 (CFO Research Services) estimated that the value of human capital represented over 36 per cent of total revenue in a typical organization.

▮ People in organizations add value and there is a case for assessing this value to provide a basis for HR planning and for monitoring the effectiveness and impact of HR policies and practices.

▮ The process of identifying measures and collecting and analysing information relating to them will focus the attention of the organization on what needs to be done to find, keep, develop and make the best use of its human capital.

▮ Measurements can be used to monitor progress in achieving strategic HR goals and generally to evaluate the effectiveness of HR practices.

▮ You cannot manage unless you measure.

However, a number of voices have advised caution about measurement. Leadbeater (2000) observed that measuring can 'result in cumbersome inventories which allow managers to manipulate perceptions of intangible values to the detriment of investors. The fact is that too few of these measures are focused on the way companies create value and make money'. Scarborough and Elias (2002) concluded from their investigations that the specific set of measures or metrics organizations reported were less important than the process of measuring and the uses for the information gathered. The Institute of Employment Studies (Hartley and Robey, 2005) emphasized that reporting on human capital is not simply about measurement. Measures on their own such as those resulting from benchmarking are not enough; they must be clearly linked to business performance 'materiality' – ie, the relevance of the measures is important. And Donkin (2005) emphasized that:

> It is not the measuring itself that is the key to successful HCM, but the intentions behind the measuring and the resulting practices that emerge. The effectiveness of these practices is heavily dependent on how they are perceived and understood by frontline employees and the kind of workplace behaviours they encourage. Measuring is not a good in itself. Adopted without any rationale it will achieve little. Its prime uses are to evaluate cost and to test the effectiveness of a strategy, pointing the way to further improvement.

HUMAN CAPITAL REPORTING

Human capital reporting is concerned with providing information on how well the human capital of an organization is managed. There are two aspects: first, external reporting to stakeholders. The second aspect is internal reporting which informs the leadership team and stakeholders about how human capital is being managed but extends this with statements of how the information will be used to guide future action. The purpose is to inform decision making about HCM not just to record the figures.

External reporting

The Accounting for People Task Force (2003) recommended that:

> The (external) report should clearly represent the Board's understanding of the links between HCM policies and practices and its business strategy and performance. This means that it should normally include details on the size and composition of the workforce, employee retention and motivation, skills, competencies and training, remuneration and fair employment practice, and leadership and succession planning. The report should follow a process that is susceptible to review by auditors, provide information in a form that enables comparison over time, and use commonly accepted terms and definitions.

Internal reporting

Internal reporting should be linked to the external reporting framework but will focus more on the practical implications of the data that has been assembled and analysed. The information and the headings of the internal report have to be tailored to the context and needs of the organization but it could:

▌ set out the quantitative and qualitative information – this might include data on the size and composition of the workforce, attraction and retention, absence, motivation, skills and competencies, learning and development activities, remuneration and fair employment practices, leadership and succession planning and the outcomes of opinion or job satisfaction surveys;

▌ analyse measures of employee satisfaction and engagement, compare them with data on business performance and demonstrate the links between them;

▌ analyse the outcomes of external benchmarking;

▌ identify the key performance drivers in the organization and indicate how HCM is contributing to adding value in each of these areas;

▮ review the extent to which people management strategy, policies and practices are contributing to the achievement of business goals;

▮ set out the returns on investments in people management and development projects and evaluate the effectiveness of the investments;

▮ draw conclusions on the implications of the data for future people management strategy, policy and practice.

DRAWING CONCLUSIONS

The conclusions drawn from the data can lead to three areas of strategic decision making: (1) the formulation and implementation of HR and business strategy; (2) the improvement of the capability of line managers in handling HR issues; (3) the overall organization of HR effort.

HR and business strategy

The importance of 'strategic relevance' is stressed by Donkin (2005). He believes that the key issue is how the information delivered by employment metrics is going to create value in the company. He suggests that 'the response must be to interpret the analysis of any body of measurement in a meaningful way set against qualitative considerations and existing management perspectives'.

To provide guidelines for action a human capital strategy can be developed making use of the data provided by human capital measurement and reporting. This will reinforce or redirect any existing HR strategies. The aim of the human capital strategy should be to inform business decisions to achieve human capital and therefore competitive advantage.

The key is to make operational the concept of 'fit' – the fit of HRM with the strategic thrust of the organization. The development of operational linkages is an important characteristic of strategic HRM. Tyson and Witcher (1994) consider that 'human resource strategies can only be studied in the context of corporate and business strategies'. HCM provides the means to create these operational linkages through fostering a resource-based strategy as described in Chapter 2.

Improving the capability of line managers in handling HR issues

The data produced by HCM can be used to provide information to line managers on how well they are handling HR issues which can initiate guidance on any improvements necessary.

The overall organization of HR effort

As explained by Ulrich and Lake (1991) 'For organizations to utilise human capital strategically, they must be organized in a manner that enables them to do so.' The data created by HCM enables organizations to come to conclusions on what should be done to improve HR effectiveness. One of the aims of HCM is to achieve 'human capital advantage' but Boxall (1996 and 1999) notes that a distinction should be made between 'human capital advantage' and 'human process advantage'. The former results from employing people with competitively valuable knowledge and skills. The latter, however, follows from the establishment of:

> … difficult to imitate, highly evolved processes within the firm, such as cross-departmental cooperation and executive development. Accordingly, 'human resource advantage', the superiority of one firm's labour management over another's, can be thought of as the product of its human capital and human process advantages.

Human process advantage is achieved by line managers in their day-to-day dealings with people, but HR has a key role to play both in developing the processes and providing guidance to managers on their implementation.

GETTING INTO ACTION

The diagnostics provided by HCM as described above are meaningless if they do not result in action. When developing measures, reporting procedures and methods of drawing conclusions it is essential at each stage to answer the following questions:

▌ *Why* are we doing this?

▌ *Where* is it leading us to?

▐ *What* sort of action do we believe can and should flow from this process?

▐ *Who* takes the action?

▐ *How* are we going to ensure that action takes place?

There are no standard answers to those questions, which is why every organization's approach to HCM will differ according to its circumstances although the basic processes of measurement and reporting will always be present.

A critical evaluation approach is used. This involves six steps:

1. Determine from the analysis the critical elements that indicate where action may be required.

2. Define the action required and by reference to the analytical data identify alternative approaches to meeting the requirement.

3. Assess the advantages and disadvantages of each approach.

4. Summarize the data and other factors influencing choice of approach.

5. Define criteria for determining the success of the selected approach.

6. Prepare the business case for the approach using the HCM data to support the proposal.

PUTTING IT ALL TOGETHER

Although the process of HCM can be described as a series of activities – measurement, reporting, analysis, evaluation, action – it can equally well be described as a holistic approach to proving the value of people and generating added value from them. Although the next part of this book describes the concept of data and the processes of measurement and reporting separately, they are all closely interrelated.

HCM could also be regarded as an attitude of mind rather than a series of techniques – a belief that investment in people is highly desirable but that it must be *considered* investment supported by evidence that a satisfactory return will be obtained from it. HCM functions as part of an integrated approach to the management of people.

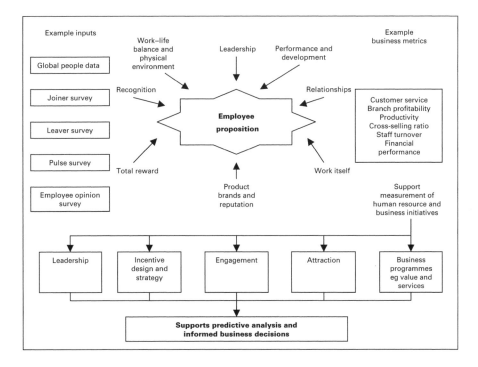

Source: IRS Employment Review 802, 18 June 2004

Figure 3.4　The Royal Bank of Scotland's human capital model

An integrated model of HCM could look like the one developed by the Royal Bank of Scotland illustrated in Figure 3.4.

This is a highly sophisticated approach to HCM but the process of HCM can still make a significant contribution to business success even when it is conducted on a much more basic level as long as the principles of measurement, reporting, analysis, evaluation and action are followed.

DEVELOPING HCM

The steps required to develop HCM are illustrated in Figure 3.5.

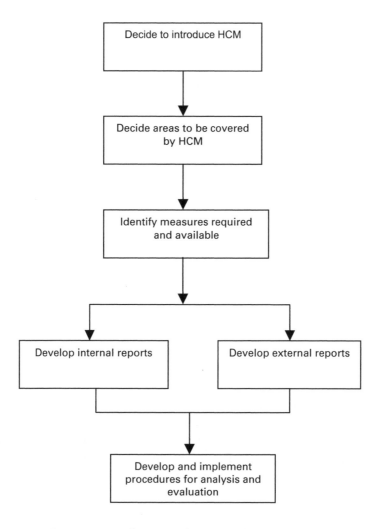

Figure 3.5 Programme for introducing HCM

The checklist below, developed by Saratoga/Pricewaterhouse-Coopers (Saratoga, 2005) and cited by IRS (2005), can be used as a guide to the development process described in more detail in the tool-kit (see the Appendix).

1. What are the priority business challenges facing your company in the next two years?

2. What human capital actions are required to maximize the opportunities required to guarantee business success?

3. How will you make those actions happen?

4. What are your KPIs [key performance indicators] and how are these related to the business challenges?

5. What data is required to measure human capital performance?

6. Are you fully informed and/or are involved in your company's OFR (now Business Review) plans?

7. What human capital information will be most useful to your shareholders and in what format?

8. What information gaps exist and how do you intend to fill them?

9. Are information systems advanced and flexible enough to respond to all recognized demands?

10. Are you satisfied that the information you produce is robust and can stand scrutiny?

11. Are you conversant with the key human capital subjects and major global trends that may be raised by shareholders?

12. Is there a direct link between what the HR function does and what the board wants it to do?

Part 2

The practice of HCM

4

Human capital data

Meaningful information on human capital relies on meaningful data. This chapter starts with an assessment of the overall considerations affecting data collection and analysis. The different types of data and the problems of collecting them are then described. The chapter continues with a guide to data management leading to brief conclusions. As explained in the last chapter, human capital data provides the starting point in the process of HCM. Data provides the basis for measures as considered in Chapter 5 and these generate the information contained in the reports discussed in Chapter 6.

OVERALL CONSIDERATIONS

Perhaps one of the reasons it has taken so long to move beyond the empty rhetoric of 'people are our most important asset' and begin to develop processes to effectively measure and report on the contribution of that asset is that there has been a perception that there is a lack of data on human capital. The HR profession must shoulder at least some of the blame for this delay. Too many times we are led to believe that collecting data and developing measures on the contribution of people to the business is too hard, too costly or too time consuming.

And yet people management and development professionals have a wealth of data at their disposal. They have data from recruitment, training, performance management, payroll and workforce opinions. They have access to data from customers, financial indicators and operations. The challenge is not in finding the data; it is in interpreting what it means.

Perhaps the easiest way to achieve this is to look for causal links. So, for example, managers might investigate whether bonus payments really do cause higher performance. There are three fundamental steps to proving causality:

▌ Establish that the cause and effect are present at the same time, for example that bonus payments are made and performance rises.

▌ Establish that the effect comes after the cause, ie that bonus payments are made before performance rises.

▌ Isolate other factors that may also cause performance to rise, eg training.

This does not need huge amounts of costly and time-consuming statistical analysis. In general, managers would rather have the answers to a few basic questions such as:

▌ What does the data tell me?

▌ What do I need to improve?

▌ What are the issues to watch?

▌ Are there any major challenges I will have that will prejudice the performance of my business unit?

▌ What investments in my human capital will generate the best return?

The Nationwide Building Society operates on these principles (CIPD, 2006a). It has developed a simple traffic-light system (illustrated in Figure 6.4), whereby senior managers can use their data to identify areas in need of attention for branch managers. The organization has achieved this by using its readily available data from four sources: HR data, employee opinion data, customer satisfaction data and business performance data. After having established a causal link between employee commitment, employee length of service and customer satisfaction, the Nationwide used some simple statistical modelling to predict the actions that would improve employee commitment and satisfaction and improve retention, therefore having impact on customer satisfaction, customer willingness to repurchase, customer willingness to recommend Nationwide products and increases in sales.

TYPES OF DATA

The main types of data as described below are business performance data, corporate social responsibility data, customer data, demographic data, development data, diversity data, employee opinion data and HR data.

Business performance data

The data that will provide information on business performance will vary from organization to organization. However, most organizations commonly collect data on sales or customer satisfaction. Other forms of data that might be used to assess business performance include productivity; incidences of cross-selling, brand recognition, customer loyalty, and in the public sector extent to which targets set by government are met.

This data even in its raw state can tell organizations something about performance, particularly if it is tracked over time or if it is compared against industry benchmarks. However, if it is correlated against employee data, such as commitment or engagement data, it can be used to calculate projected financial returns on improvement in employee satisfaction, commitment or loyalty.

The Nationwide Building Society, for example, conducts an extensive member survey that informs its business simulations to predict the value of a particular course of action. Pfizer uses a number of key performance indicators to track business activity, including monitoring the number of sales calls made (CIPD, 2006a).

Corporate social responsibility (CSR) data

CSR data is growing in importance to organizations. Environment is one of the specific reporting areas mentioned in the Business Review, introduced as part of the EU Accounts Modernisation Directive, but even before this came into force many organizations were reporting on CSR issues. CSR data is demanded more and more by customers who want higher ethical standards from business in the way in which organizations treat labour, particularly in the developing world, and their record on environmental issues. Several of the organizations interviewed for this book incorporate CSR as part of their reporting process and some feed human capital information into the CSR reporting process.

CSR data can be correlated against customer data to see if improving the organization's record is likely to result in increased sales. It can also be correlated against employee data to see if it increases the number of applicants for jobs (because they see the organizations as fair and just), levels of commitment and satisfaction or organizational loyalty.

Customer data

Customer data is an important source of business performance data (see above) and also an important source of data in its own right. By collecting data on customer opinions and perceptions organizations can become more informed about the kind of behaviours they need to encourage in their employees, the type of sales techniques that will give most value and the products and services that customers are likely to demand in the future.

This information will need to be viewed in the light of financial data. Customers will obviously be delighted with more free services but this may not be a valid financial proposition!

Raw customer data will give information about the customer base, but again will need to be correlated against other forms of data before the real information is gleaned. So does an increase in customer satisfaction results in an increase in sales? We may assume this is the case but it is not always going to be so. Customer data can also indicate desirable targets for employee behaviour or services processes.

Some of the organizations interviewed for this book use sophistic-ated customer opinion surveys which they then correlate against other forms of data to provide information on the nature and type of service they should be providing and the skills their employees need to deliver this. Standard Chartered Bank uses customer satisfaction as one of its business outcomes and both Norwich Union and Pfizer mentioned that they specifically track customer activity and feed this into their human capital information processes (CIPD, 2006a).

Demographic data

Most organizations, and certainly all those interviewed for this book, collect some form of demographic data. This includes data on age, length of service, ethnicity and male to female ratios.

This data is used in a number of ways. Some use it to compare their workforce profile with the national labour market profile to identify any potential problems. At the Ministry of Defence, for example, managers began to express concern that so many senior members of staff were over 45. However, when they compared their profile against the demographic profile nationally and future trends, they began to understand that they are likely to be increasingly dependent on older workers and so actively engage in both recruiting and developing older workers. Other organizations interviewed use this data to get a better understanding of how they might address their 'hard to fill' vacancies and to access information on the external labour market to see who else is fishing in the same labour pool and whether there are enough people with the profile they are looking for to fill the gaps. This can then enable them to decide whether they need to revise their person specifications or look at alternative labour markets to fill their vacancies.

However, while recognizing that this basic data is needed to provide a profile of the workforce and as a benchmark of diversity, some of those interviewed questioned the use of this form of data for HCM and whether it really added value to human capital evaluation. Certainly in its raw state the data is open to misinterpretation. However, as later chapters will discuss, even very basic data can provide a good starting point to developing better understanding of human capital issues.

Development data

The competencies and skills of the workforce are often presented as a basic component of human capital and yet not everyone interviewed collected data on training and development. However, most did, and the kinds of data collected included the number of training events held, training days per employee, and registered users of online learning programmes, etc.

One human capital manager told us that their primary concern is capability, '... do people have the skills and competence to do the job and if so how can we prove it?' Others also said that they collect development data to ensure that people are fit for the job. However, it was also said that development data is linked to attracting and retaining talent. A key element of training data for many was about assessing the gaps and identifying the training needs of individuals to be moved into key positions. In this way development data was also linked to succession planning and career management.

At Standard Chartered Bank a key emphasis of human capital is about growing its talent pipeline by both attracting and retaining talent and accelerating the progression and development of the best talent. For Standard Chartered Bank, this is a key source of data to inform human capital evaluation (CIPD, 2006a). Other organizations use development data to provide information on skills used and future skills requirements and skills gaps.

However, the key for most of the people interviewed was about measuring the effect of training on future performance. This is difficult but not impossible and emphasizes the close link between development and performance management. A number of factors will need to be considered when attempting to correlate data, including:

▌ the extent to which individuals have the opportunity to apply what they have learnt in their current jobs;

▌ whether training is improving their capability in their current job or preparing them for a future role;

▌ the criteria against which performance is assessed and the extent to which individuals can influence these criteria.

Diversity data

Some organizations are required to collect diversity data, and this is considered good practice in order to avoid accusations of discrimination. Most of the organizations interviewed collected diversity data under the umbrella of demographic data, collecting information on age, sex, race and disability. But some felt it was a more major issue. For example, Standard Chartered Bank acquires data on equality of access to development opportunities.

There is some evidence that reflecting the diversity of the customer base in the workforce can enhance business performance and diversity data could be correlated against customer data and business performance data to test this in practice.

Employee opinion data

Employee opinion data is the most common way that organizations assess levels of satisfaction, engagement, commitment and loyalty. The people and performance model developed by Purcell and his team at Bath University (Purcell *et al*, 2003) identified these issues as significant drivers of discretionary effort and hence business performance.

Some examples of the types of employee opinion data collected are:

▌ workforce climate surveys;

▌ leadership surveys;

▌ 360-degree appraisal feedback;

▌ performance appraisal feedback;

▌ employee engagement surveys;

▌ culture surveys;

▌ attitude surveys.

For Standard Chartered Bank this is particularly a key issue. The bank has been measuring employee engagement for some time and now achieves a 97 per cent response rate from among 40,000 people in 56 countries. Internal research has now established that better engaged business units outperform those with low levels of engagement.

The Royal Bank of Scotland surveys all employees across the group and has achieved an 84 per cent response rate. The bank measures its results against the ISR Global Financial Services Norm and the ISR Global High-Performance Norm, as well as using the results to inform leadership development programmes.

The Nationwide Building Society also uses its employee opinion data to feed into the scenario modelling which enables managers to predict the likely financial impact of different courses of action in terms of people management (CIPD, 2006a).

HR data

Finally, data on the various activities and aspects of HR is routinely collected by all of the practitioners interviewed. The kinds of HR data collected and used for human capital evaluation and reporting purposes included:

▌ monitoring operating costs per head;

▌ revenue/profit per employee;

- monitoring absence rates;

- permanent to temporary staff ratio;

- average salary;

- reward differentiation based on performance contribution and potential;

- recruitment figures: length of time to recruit, number of applicants for each job, skill level of applicants, etc;

- ratio of internal to external recruitment;

- health and safety data;

- data from exist interviews;

- performance management or appraisal data;

- employee turnover and retention.

Turnover and retention is one of the key measures used by most organizations. It is particularly attractive data as it is usually relatively easy to attach costs to it and therefore to calculate the savings if turnover can be improved. One HR director reported that he got the full attention of his executive management team when he told them a 1 per cent reduction in turnover would equate with a new BMW for each of them!

However, the approach to the calculation of turnover differs from organization to organization, which makes comparison difficult. Another difficulty is that in some industries, or even some parts of the workplace, turnover is low and likely to remain so for cultural rather than people management reasons.

So, for example, whereas large public sector organizations are primarily using data to inform them about skill shortages, Standard Chartered Bank is tracking vulnerable groups to ensure the flow of talent, Centrica monitors new starters to identify critical stages where people are mostly likely to leave and the Royal Bank of Scotland looks at the geographical distribution of its employees, monitoring external factors that have an impact on turnover (CIPD, 2006a). Many other organizations saw this as more of a resourcing issue to ensure enough people in the right place at the right time to deliver business objectives.

Apart from turnover and retention data, much of the data listed above does not tell organizations very much in its raw state. However, when analysed and assessed with other forms of data it can be very informative. For example, the work at Bath University was able to identify significant links between various HR processes and levels of commitment, satisfaction and loyalty. They found that when people felt fairly treated by the performance management process, or were able to balance their work and home commitments, or believed that there was a genuine interest in their career progression, they also felt a high level, of commitment and satisfaction, which in turn tended to raise their levels of discretionary effort (defined as the extra effort people put into their job over and above the necessary minimum).

Similarly, absence data is collected by most organizations, probably as a result of the number of surveys highlighting the costs of absenteeism. However, yet again organizations take a different approach to the data. Some keep it to monitor and identify problems with particular individuals who have high levels of absence. Others use the figures as an indicator of more serious underlying problems.

The next chapter will deal with analysis and measurement of data but some of the ways HR data can be used to evaluate and monitor human capital include:

▎ using performance management data to inform capability or competence levels;

▎ assessing performance, training and career intentions data to develop succession plans;

▎ comparing health and safety data with training of performance data;

▎ assessing recruitment figures with performance data to get more accurate figures for the cost of ongoing vacancies, for example by monitoring the effects on existing staff;

▎ looking for correlations between data such as absence rates and recruitment problems, health and safety and poor levels of commitment or job satisfaction, numbers of temporary staff and levels of performance or turnover and training.

PROBLEMS WITH DATA COLLECTION

A number of problems with the collection of data were identified from discussion with practitioners and others. Perhaps the most problematic situation is when companies merge. This often results in two very different sets of data collected using different techniques and different calculations, which makes it more difficult to assess trends or to establish historical knowledge. The second most common problem occurred in diverse organizations possibly using different HR information systems where information is collected and reported in different ways.

This latter problem is particularly acute in diverse organizations operating in many different business areas. One such organization graphically illustrated the problem by relating how even simple statistics such as headcount could not be relied upon because the different systems used in different parts of the business calculated the figure using different formulas.

However, such problems are not insurmountable as members of the CIPD Human Capital Panel demonstrate. The Royal Bank of Scotland, for example, collects data from all parts of the business around the world using numerous different systems. By interpreting this in a standardized form the bank is still able to generate very quickly meaningful information to inform both its business and people management activities (CIPD, 2006a).

To deal with these problems HR people need to become more statistically competent and better able to express what they want from technology in terms of the nature of the data they need and how this needs to be presented. Although they do not have to be experts in statistics (the issues of HR skills for HCM will be discussed in Chapter 9) they will need at least to be able to understand what the different methods of collecting data mean when it comes to its interpretation and analysis.

In addition, many of the practitioners interviewed thought that the problems associated with collecting data from HR information systems stemmed from the lack of HR involvement in the specification of these systems when they were developed. As a result HR was often sold systems that did not entirely fulfil its need to provide useful information to inform people management strategies.

A GUIDE TO DATA MANAGEMENT

The summary of the kinds of data that have an input to HCM demonstrate that there are a number of levels on which organizations operate with regard to data collection and management.

The model in Table 4.1 illustrates this and offers some guidance for organizations starting out on the process of generating human capital data. The model emphasizes that it is important to start with the basics. If an organization cannot inform the outside world accurately how many employees it has, it cannot expect any reliance or trust to be placed in any data it generates.

The basic steps for the generation of good quality human capital data are as follows:

1. Start with basic data and analysis restricted to identifying trends and patterns and what they mean.

2. Demonstrate its integrity by ensuring that it is accurate, reliable and of value.

3. Progress to higher levels of data collection, demonstrate the values of particular processes and enable managers to see how their actions can impact on performance.

4. Identify the drivers of business performance.

The aim of the data collection process should be to create a virtuous cycle where improved people management results from meaningful data provided to line managers that enables thoughtful insight and credibility for recommended management actions. Over time, this will create a new environment in which the HR function is a provider of knowledge and an enabler of good people management leading to improved business performance.

The model in Figure 4.1 depicts this cycle. It identifies the steps required to reach a stage in the evaluation and reporting of human capital data where the HR function is making a real contribution to the understanding of what drives bottom-line improvement.

CONCLUSIONS

In its raw form many types of data routinely collected by HR departments can be informative and the most basic data can reveal insights into the contribution and value of human capital, making it worth the effort of collecting and recording. Even crude data can give a lot of statistical information that can be very persuasive when backed up with argument to chief executives or senior managers of the value

Table 4.1   Levels of data collection

	Level		
	Basic	**Intermediate**	**Higher**
Action	• Collect basic input data, eg absence, employee turnover • Identify useful data already available such as data from pay reviews, performance management, job evaluation, training, the recruitment process • Use this data to communicate essential information to managers about absence, turnover or accident levels, compared by department • Look for trends or patterns in the data and investigate their causes	• Design data collection for specific human capital needs. For example, conduct an employee attitude survey to measure satisfaction, or follow up on training activity to monitor implementation and use • Use this data to inform the design and implementation of people management policies and processes • Look for correlations between data – for example whether high levels of job satisfaction occur when certain HR practices are in place, such as performance management, career management or flexible working • Communicate the value of processes to line managers and identify specific actions to improve people management	• Identify key performance indicators relating to the business strategy, and design and implement data collection processes to measure against them • Feed both quantitative and qualitative information into an analysis model such as a balanced scorecard • Provide managers with indicators on a range of measures designed to inform them on performance and progress in their department • Accompany this with specific actions to be taken informed by the resulting human capital data • Interpret and communicate data in ways that will be meaningful to a range of audiences
Outcome	• Measures of efficiency and effectiveness • Basic information for managers on headcount, make-up of the workforce, and so on • Identification of any action that might be needed as a result of these measures – for example to reduce accident rates, to improve the diversity profile of the workforce or to reduce absence	• Measures of process • Information to help design the HR model that is most likely to contribute to performance • Communication to managers not just how to implement processes but with accompanying information on why they are important and what they can achieve	• Identification of the drivers of business performance • Information that will enable better-informed decision making both internally on the management of people and externally on the progress with regard to strategy

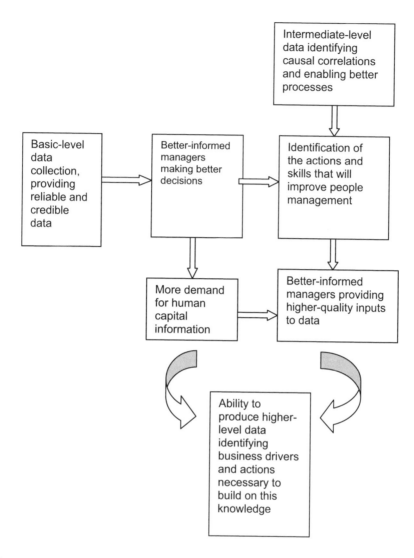

Figure 4.1 The data collection cycle

of human capital. However, the real information comes when data is correlated or compared. In its most simple form this might mean looking for patterns or asking a series of questions:

▌ Are absence rates high in departments where there are large numbers of job vacancies or it is taking a long time to fill vacancies?

▌ Are there more accidents in parts of the business where more temporary staff are employed?

▮ Are most people leaving the business just when they have completed a certain level of training?

▮ Does retention improve when more vacancies are filled by internal applicants?

▮ Does profit/revenue per employee rise when there is additional training spend?

At a more sophisticated level steps can be taken to correlate different data to identify if there is a cause and effect taking place. However, the most useful information comes when modelling techniques are applied to enable the identification of business drivers. This will be discussed in later chapters.

Perhaps the most important point to make when it comes to human capital data is that in itself it may be interesting but it is the actions attached to it that makes it valuable. The goal of human capital data generation should be to provide managers with information informing them of the best people management actions to take which in turn raises performance and drives business improvement and competitiveness.

This should result in a virtuous circle where: good HR = better data = thoughtful insight = credibility = a new environment, and where HR gets placed at the decision-making tables and is relied upon to provide meaningful and insightful information to inform action.

However, this will only happen if the data that HR is able to generate is material, reliable and trustworthy and has meaning for managers. It is essential therefore that the data is continuously reviewed and assessed to make sure that it is credible and robust. Managers are unlikely to act on the data if they don't believe it or if it is continuously undermined by other information available to them.

5

Measuring human capital

HCM is concerned with proving the value of people – assessing the impact of HRM practices and the contribution of people to bottom-line performance. Methods of measuring impact and contribution based upon human capital data have therefore to be developed, which is what this chapter is about. The chapter starts with a general discussion of measurement issues and an analysis of the different types of measures. Consideration is next given to the process of developing measures and approaches to analysis. A description of the main analytical models follows and the chapter ends with a number of examples of approaches to measurement.

MEASUREMENT ISSUES

Research by the Chartered Management Institute in 2006 (Scott-Jackson *et al*, 2006) found that 86 per cent of directors agreed that they value their employees as key assets and 77 per cent believe that their workforce development is aligned to business goals. However, only 68 per cent measure the contribution made by employees.

Measurement difficulties

Measurement is notoriously difficult because the things that human capital is likely to influence such as customer satisfaction, innovation and service delivery are at the mercy of numerous other contextual factors. Whereas is can be relatively easy to collect data to describe the workforce and the prevalence of certain practices, particularly where sophisticated HR information systems exist, it is more difficult to develop credible and reliable measures and decide what the measures will tell us.

In terms of human capital evaluation and reporting, measurement can be viewed in a number of ways. Chapter 4 looked at the kinds of data that can be used to develop a better understanding of human capital. Generally we find that organizations are more comfortable talking about data than they are about measures. However, if data is going to tell us anything meaningful it has to be considered in the context of measurement.

One of the reasons why measurement is difficult is that human capital is not owned by the organization but secured through the employment relationship. Many of the things that could give us an indication of the contribution of people are out of the control of the business. Employees can decide how much effort above the absolute minimum required to retain their job they put into their work; this is sometimes called discretionary effort. To secure the extra effort from their employees that will really make a difference to their business, organizations must identify the triggers that will encourage this discretionary effort. This argument is discussed comprehensively in the report produced by Purcell and his colleagues in Bath University based on their research (Purcell *et al*, 2003).

Human capital therefore represents the fit between the demand for and supply of human capabilities. Firms will not value and therefore not measure aspects of employee behaviour or capability that they cannot use in the pursuit of their business objectives. At firm level, therefore, the contribution of human capital is contingent on the supply and relevance of employee competencies to the business needs of the organization as determined by its strategy. This context-dependent quality makes it impossible to identify a standard set of measures that will be relevant and applicable in all circumstances.

In reality there are a number of measures that are commonly used, but important distinctions can be made between measurement and data as discussed below.

Measurement and data

Measurement can be regarded as a way of analysing and interpreting data that already exists. For example, if a measure of organizational capability is a desirable outcome, then performance management data, training data or skills data may be used to achieve this. In this case, how the existing data is used and interpreted rather than how it is collected will determine the outcome measure.

In some cases the data itself may be an outcome of measurement. For example, data on absenteeism is usually the result of an effort to measure absenteeism. This means that a definition has to be produced of what constitutes absence, for example:

▌ How is sick leave categorized? For example, some employers count time off for booked hospital appointments as absence and some do not.

▌ What about unauthorized leave?

▌ Is time off to care for a sick dependent classed as absence? Some organizations allow a certain amount of paid dependent's leave and some do not.

▌ Is maternity leave recorded as absence?

These are the kinds of questions that need to be asked to determine the measure of absence that is going to result in absence data, and the decisions made will affect what is counted as absence and what is not. This means that the data may vary considerably depending on the measure – the same things may not have been measured to give absence data. This gives rise to problems when comparing across different parts of the organizations or against other organizations.

Measures are therefore important in determining how data is collected and also how it is used. It is not surprising, given that there are these different ways of looking at measurement, that the measurement and analysis of data are often inseparable and sometimes become confused in the search for meaningful human capital information.

CLASSIFICATION OF MEASURES

The three basic classifications of measures as identified by Kearns (2005a) are:

▌ *Activity measures* – these simply record the level of activity such as the number of training days per employee. They do not assess the quality of the activity, for example the impact the training has made on performance.

▌ *Performance measures* – these assess performance improvements in such terms as contribution, productivity and profitability.

▌ *Added value measures* – these assess the extent to which the measured value of the contribution of people exceeds the cost of generating it. ROI (return on investment) or return on capital employed measures can be broadly included in this category.

The distinction between these classifications is important. Added value measures are the most revealing followed by performance measures. Activity measures are often the only ones available but they do not give any indication of the outcomes of the activity which means that they are less valuable than the others.

DEVELOPING MEASURES

Research commissioned by the CIPD and carried out by Scarborough and Elias of Warwick University (Scarborough and Elias, 2002) found that it is not what organizations decide to measure that is important but the process of measurement itself. As they noted:

> In short, measures are less important that the activity of measuring – of continuously developing and refining our understanding of the productive role of human capital within particular settings, by embedding such activities in management practices, and linking them to the business strategy of the firm.

This sentiment is echoed by Donkin (2005), when he says: 'It is not the measuring itself that is the key to successful human capital management but the intentions behind the measuring and the resulting practices that emerge.'

Measures therefore are not an end in themselves but rather are a means to inform and test strategy, evaluate costs and assess the impacts of different actions.

Approaches to measurement

Among the practitioners interviewed for this book and in the literature a number of approaches to measurement can be discerned. Centrica (CIPD, 2006a) differs from others by deliberately starting the organization's journey towards HC evaluation and reporting with an attempt to identify the measures that would be of value to its business model. This was done by conducting a high-level review of its business and people strategy – what it was that the business was trying to achieve and what human factors would act as either blockers or drivers. Decisions were then made about what would need to be measured to monitor progress. The aim was to create a simple series of measures that would be easy to understand, would help to drive changes in behaviours and would support the strategic aims of the business. As a result Centrica identified eight key measures, four of which are financial while the other four are more traditionally people focused:

∎ human capital return on investment;

∎ training return on investment;

∎ cost of absence;

∎ costs of leavers (resignations);

∎ employee engagement;

∎ annual pay audits;

∎ employee share scheme/flex benefits;

∎ diversity and inclusion.

Only when it had established the measures did Centrica set out to identify what data would be required and from which sources. The approach has therefore been very much driven by business strategy, people issues and measurement requirements rather than the availability of data. A common framework of measurement is used for both internal and external reporting processes. This allows the company to have a full set of measures to drive improvement and change within the business while allowing a subset of the information to be published externally to meet business reporting requirements. The seven 'must ask' questions identified by Centrica are:

1. What is the business unit strategic agenda? 3 months? 6 months? 12 months? Beyond?

2. What are the key people issues driving/blocking the strategic agenda?

3. For each people issue, what would be a successful outcome – ie what would 'good' look like?

4. What information do we need to show that we have achieved 'good'?

   ▮ How often?

   ▮ How detailed?

   ▮ How accurate?

   ▮ How should it be used to drive action?

5. Where will the data come from?

6. How will the information be analysed/presented?

7. Who is going to drive this?

Standard Chartered Bank also started at the strategic level when it came to designing measures (CIPD, 2006a). The organization's starting point for the development of metrics was to identify people levers for the achievement of business strategy and then to formulate these people levers into a series of questions designed to inform progress against them. The bank has deliberately avoided reporting on data that is readily available but does not address the strategic business questions identified. The intention is to evolve the bank's scorecard over time as currently there are some measures it would like to include but cannot because their reliability cannot be guaranteed.

The Accounting for People Task force identified six key measures that seem to be used most commonly by companies. These are:

▮ the profile of the workforce;

▮ workforce turnover;

▮ retention rates;

▮ workforce absenteeism;

▮ performance and productivity;

▮ engagement.

The Chartered Management Institute research published in 2006 proposes a three-tier approach to measures, involving:

▌ Basic measures which include quantitative data and employee profile statistics and are crucial for understanding the basic make-up of the workforce but not sufficient to drive action to assess human capital in relation to strategic goals.

▌ Standard comparable analytic measures which include comparable quantitative data indicating the extent of workforce contribution to performance and which are defined to provide useful actionable information. Such measures may be predefined and applicable to all types of organizations.

▌ Strategic HCM measures – measures of strategic alignment which cannot be predetermined and have to be developed for each organization's particular strategic context.

A review of the available case studies on human capital measurement revealed another five measures that are also popular:

▌ added value per employee;

▌ profit or revenue per employee;

▌ reward strategy;

▌ leadership and succession planning/talent management;

▌ the cost and/or effectiveness of training;

▌ the link to bottom-line indicators.

Another desirable feature of human capital measures is that it should be possible to link them to bottom-line indicators. For those whose starting point for human capital evaluation and reporting is at the strategic level the link is implicit. For others who choose to take a more pragmatic approach the process of linking to the bottom line tends to be more evolutionary.

The Nationwide Building Society has taken a practical stance on the collection of data and development of measures. To build its human capital model the organization used data that was already there – even if it was not perfect for the job. Executives wanted data that would be available in the future and that would enable them to make a case to ask for more tailored data from managers. They recognized that there were a number of areas they either did not measure or could do better such as leadership. Although they had existing key bottom-line performance indicators these were not based on the human capital model. However, they hoped that by a process of evolution and building the case for human capital they would improve their measures and include human capital measures in the bottom-line indicators in the future.

For Cameron McKenna, a medium-sized law firm in the City of London, it was the building blocks of the firm's strategy that drove the need to measure performance. This firm too used readily available data and evolved a number of existing key performance indicators into defined human capital reporting. Again, the firm intends to evolve these over time as more strategy-related programmes are developed and new measures became available (CIPD, 2006a).

Centrica is using a common framework of measurement for both internal and external measures at a strategic level. This allows executives to have a full set of detailed measures to drive improvement and change within the business while allowing a subset of the information to be published externally for the Business Review. The organization is also developing a series of internal measures on tactical and operational levels to address issues such as cost, quality, efficiency and resource utilization per transaction in the HR Shared Services unit. This series of measures is driving the definition of new and revised key performance indicators all of which have a direct link to bottom-line business indicators.

APPROACHES TO ANALYSIS

Analysis is concerned with understanding and interpreting the meaning of data, whether or not that data has been collected using specified measures. As discussed in the previous chapter, even rather crude data can be useful if it gives an indication of a real or potential problems or can be used to identify trends over time. Many of the people interviewed were using quite simple forms of analysis to gather information from their data. Most argued that they didn't want to over-analyse and overload their information systems with too much detail.

Again, absence rates can be an example. Raw data on absence will identify very quickly individuals or departments who have particularly high levels of absence. However, to give really meaning-ful data, we must first be confident that this data has been collected against the same measures in all circumstances. If we then analyse the data by comparing with or against other data, we can begin to interpret some of the causes of absence and hence identify actions that might reduce it. For example, absence may be high in departments where there are a lot of vacancies or where turnover is also high. This would prompt an investigation to establish whether the failure to fill vacancies is the cause of absenteeism because people are stressed by having to cover for vacant jobs, or whether management issues are causing the problem. Depending on the outcome of the investigation a decision might be made to improve the recruitment process, redesign jobs to make them easier to fill, invest in management training or restructure the department.

ANALYTICAL MODELS

A number of models can be used to analyse human capital information to produce meaningful information for the business both internally and externally. A number of the most commonly used are reviewed below with an assessment of their benefits and limitations.

Balanced scorecard

The balanced scorecard, or at least tailored versions of it, is perhaps one of the best-known models and most commonly used of all the analytical models,

The original balanced scorecard was developed by Kaplan and Norton (1996) and was designed to counter the tendency of companies to focus on short-term financial reporting. The scorecard, as illustrated in Figure 5.1, originally had four elements – financial, customer, the internal business process, and learning and growth.

The model presents each element within a system representing multiple objectives as a basis for setting targets. For example, under the financial element, the scorecard asks: 'To succeed financially, how should we appear to our shareholders?'; and under the customer element, it asks: 'To achieve our vision, how should we appear to our customers?' Some organizations have replaced the learning and growth element with a broader 'people' category, which allows them a wider perspective on which to judge performance.

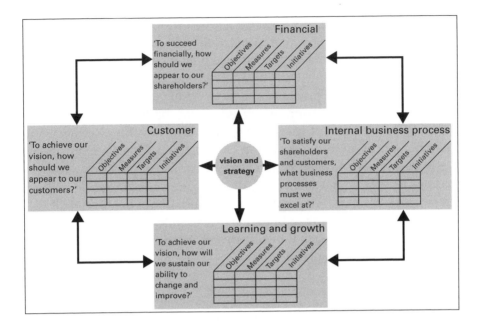

Source: After Kaplan, R S and Norton, D P (1992 and 1996)

Figure 5.1   The balanced scorecard framework

Benefits

The major benefit of the balanced scorecard is that it allows people issues to be considered alongside and equal to financial and other business considerations. It can provide a simple communication tool enabling graphic illustrations of performance for both internal and external audiences. It also aligns the evaluation of the people dimension to the organization's strategic aims.

Limitations

Some organizations have been tempted to over-engineer the number of metrics used which can result in confusion and the recipients of the data becoming swamped with measures and targets so that they lose their meaning. Also, because it focuses on target setting, the balanced scorecard is driven by the context and while it can be a useful tool for internal reporting and communication it does not have much relevance for external or industry reporting because it gives little basis for comparison.

The Human Capital Monitor

Mayo (2001) has attempted to identify the human value of the enterprise or 'human asset worth'. He argues that people should be viewed as assets rather than costs. The model focuses on three main areas:

▌ how an organization should recognize the intrinsic diversity in the worth of its people and value it;

▌ how to create a framework of people-related metrics as part of an organization's overall performance;

▌ how to quantify both the financial and non-financial value to stakeholders.

The Human Capital Monitor provides a formula for calculating the human asset worth of individual employees, which is shown in Figure 5.2 below.

The human asset worth is therefore defined as being equal to 'employment cost × individual asset multiplier (IAM)/1,000'. This is a weighted average assessment of capability, potential to grow, personal performance (contribution) and alignment to the organization's values set in the context of the workforce environment (ie how leadership, culture, motivation and learning are driving success).

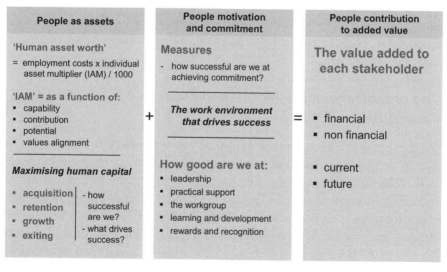

Source: Mayo, A (2001)

Figure 5.2   The Human Capital Monitor

Because this model is designed to be tailored to the individual needs of the organization it is not the absolute figure that is important. But rather the process of measurement leads you to consider whether human capital is sufficient, increasing or decreasing and highlights issues to address.

Mayo stresses that success with the model is more likely if organizations focus on a few relevant enterprise-wide measures that are critical in creating shareholder value or achieving current and future organizational goals, rather than trying to use too many measures.

Benefits

The main strength of the Human Capital Monitor is that is can put a price tag on the value and contribution of individuals to the business. Many of the practitioners interviewed for this book stressed that being able to put pound signs in front of human capital is a powerful tool in winning the support of senior managers.

Limitations

The model rests on the ability to calculate the capability, contribution, potential and values alignment of people. Although many organizations are making strenuous efforts to collective data in these areas, with the possible exception of contribution, many of these assessments are still largely subjective, thus severely limiting the validity of the final figure. Also, by focusing so heavily on the measure of human asset worth the model tends to neglect the accompanying actions or strategies to develop this worth.

The organizational performance model – Mercer HR Consulting

In the early 1990s, Mercer HR Consulting assembled a research group of labour/organizational economists and work psychologists to develop methods to measure the business impact of human capital practices in organizations. The group began by conducting a review and assessment of documented empirical research on the workforce drivers of organizational productivity. The review encompassed hundreds of studies in economics, psychology, communications and general management, covering more than 1,000 organizations. The work led to a model that explicitly linked HCM to organizational performance and, ultimately, shareholder value.

According to the model depicted in Figure 5.3, a firm's human capital strategy consists of six interconnected factors:

▮ *people* – who is in the organization; their skills and competencies on hiring; what skills and competences they develop through training and experience; their level of qualification; and the extent to which they apply firm-specific or generalized human capital;

▮ *work processes* – how work gets done; the degree of teamwork and interdependence among organizational units; and the role of technology;

▮ *managerial structure* – the degree of employee discretion, management direction and control; spans of control, performance management and work procedures;

▮ *information and knowledge* – how information is shared and exchanged among employees and with suppliers and customers through formal or informal means;

▮ *decision making* – how important decisions are made and who makes them; the degree of decentralization, participation and timeliness of decisions;

▮ *rewards* – how monetary and non-monetary incentives are used; how much pay is at risk; individual versus group rewards; current versus longer-term 'career rewards'.

In many organizations the elements have evolved and in practice there is no explicit human capital strategy. Where this is the case there is real potential to misalign the various components of the model which will indicate that human capital is not being optimized. This in turn means there are real opportunities for substantial improvement in returns if there is effective measurement of the organization's human capital assets and the management practices that affect their performance.

Benefits

Encourages organizations to look at all the factors that combine to impact on the contribution of people to business performance. If organizations also buy in to some of the statistical tools marketed by Mercer, they can measure their performance against the model, identify gaps and hence areas for improvement.

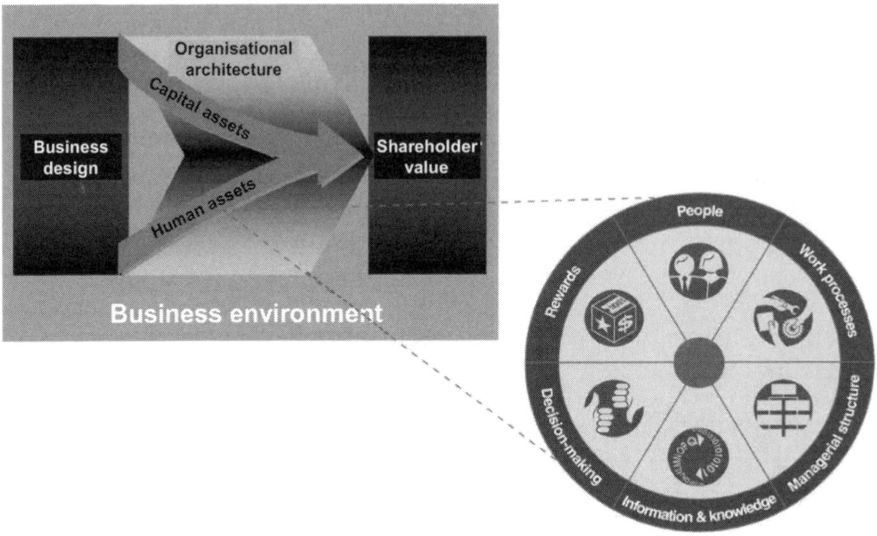

Source: Mercer Human Resource Consulting (2004)

Figure 5.3　The Mercer organizational performance model

Limitations

Like most of the available models, outcomes will be entirely dependent on the context in which the organizational performance model is applied and it assumes that a certain level of information will be available. Many organizations would not yet be in a position to apply this model effectively.

The Human Capital Index

The Human Capital Index® is marketed by Watson Wyatt Worldwide. It is based on a survey of both US and European companies linking their key management practices to their market value and shareholder value creation with evidence of critical HR practices. The survey concluded that four major categories of HR practice could be linked to a 30 per cent increase in shareholder value, as detailed in Table 5.1.

The four critical practices are:

▌ *Clear rewards and accountability* that differentiate between high and poor performers.

▌ *A collegial and flexible workplace environment* encouraging teamwork and cooperation.

Table 5.1   The Human Capital Index

Practice	Impact on market value
Total rewards and accountability	16.5%
Collegial, flexible workplace	9.0%
Recruiting and retention excellence	7.9%
Communication integrity	7.1%

Source: Watson Wyatt Worldwide (2002)

▌ *A commitment* to hiring and retaining the best people and development of recruitment practices to support the firm's strategic aims.

▌ *A level of integrity* in communication strategy where goals are clearly stated and business processes have a high level of transparency.

Benefits

The model provides support for the concept that better people management practices will result in better business performance.

Limitations

The index focuses on a 'best practice' concept of value adding HR policies and does not help organizations to identify the policies that will work best in their particular contextual circumstances. It is also open to criticism because it fails to demonstrate that these practices lead to high performance (ie demonstrating causality and direction).

People management and business performance – the engagement model

The application of the engagement model that has been most widely publicized relates to research at Sears Roebuck (Rucci *et al*, 1998) which looked at the employee–customer–profit chain (see Figure 5.4). In essence, the theory states that if you keep your employees satisfied, they will help ensure that your customers remain satisfied, and your customers in turn will ensure and improve your corporate profits. Sears Roebucks' demonstration of these relationships have been replicated in the UK in a number of organizations, including the Nationwide Building Society.

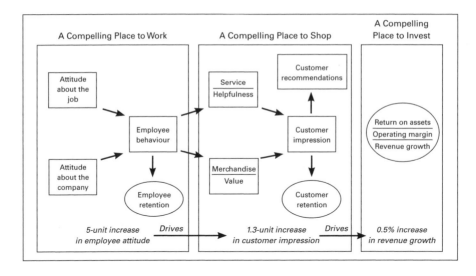

Source: After Rucci *et al* (1998)

Figure 5.4   The employee–customer–profit chain

This model has supported the view that high levels of employee satisfaction or engagement will result in better customer services, more satisfied customers and hence more repeat business or cross-selling. The result is that the pursuit of employee satisfaction and engagement has become interlinked with the concept of HR strategy and business alignment. Measuring and improving employee satisfaction for some companies, particularly in the retailing and service sectors, has therefore become an important basis of organizational improvement. Employee attitude or climate surveys have become a key measure of human capital, with a strong emphasis being placed on them in companies such as Marks & Spencer and Asda.

Other organizations, such as Standard Chartered Bank and the Royal Bank of Scotland have shown demonstrable links between employee morale or attitudes and a variety of business metrics, particularly at the business unit performance level (including shrinkage, absenteeism, employee theft and customer profitability).

The Bath people and performance model

The theory that better motivated, satisfied, loyal and committed employees would deliver higher performance was further explored in research commissioned by the CIPD from Bath University (Purcell *et al*, 2002). The CIPD asked the research team to investigate the relationship between people management and business performance. The resulting model (see Figure 5.5) demonstrates that a variety of HR practices contribute to higher levels of ability, motivation and opportunity among individual employees.

However, the model also shows that a number of other factors, such as the role of frontline management, and the extent to which they are

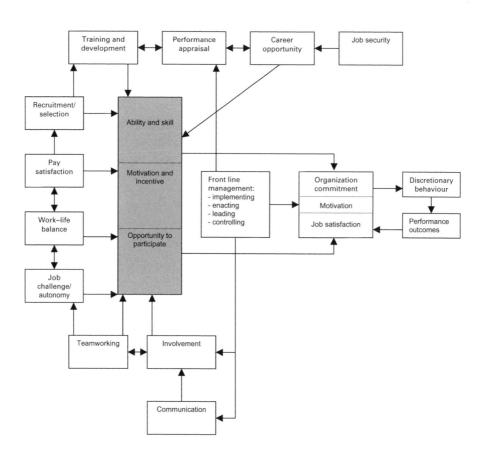

Source: Purcell *et al* (2003)

Figure 5.5 People and Performance Model

embedded values were important if this 'AMO' is to have an effect on business outcomes. 'AMO' is defined as:

∎ the *ability* to perform;

∎ the *motivation* to use the ability to perform;

∎ the *opportunity* to apply abilities in ways in which the organization will benefit.

Benefits

The engagement model is easily understandable, can be applied in any circumstances and allows organizations to assess their policies and practices in a structured way.

Limitations

A number of factors associated with successful engagement are difficult to influence in the short term and therefore measurement of human capital contribution is hindered by the time lag required for action to take place.

Newbury Index Rating (NIR)

The NIR is a measure developed by Kearns (as reported by Thomas in *Personnel Today*, 2005). The rating is based on viewing the organization from a number of perspectives with the aim of producing a measure that clearly indicates how well the organization is managing to capitalize on the value of its people. The questions the NIR asks as a basis for rating are:

1. Who is your dedicated HR strategist and does that person have a full seat at board level?

2. Can you demonstrate a value-added performance improvement from all of your employees over the past 12 months?

3. Does all your training expenditure produce an acceptable return on investment?

4. What methodology do you use to answer question 3?

5. Does your organization have a clearly defined and effective learning system in operation?

6. What is your projected added value (in monetary terms) from HCM practices over the next three years?

7. What methods do your employees use to improve the value you receive from your supply chain?

8. If you use a balanced scorecard, or similar management model, do you have a discrete measurement for 'people' measures? If so, provide examples.

9. Do you clearly distinguish between activity, performance and added value measures?

10. What system do you have in place to capture added-value ideas from employees?

Benefits

The list of questions upon which the rating is based is searching and comprehensive.

Limitations

Only organizations with very sophisticated measurement processes will be able to answer many of the questions.

The Human Capital Report

The Human Capital Report (originally referred to as the Human Capital Index) developed by Lees (2004) is a number out of 100 that is an individual and group measure of human capital based on the mean performance scores from 360-degree feedback for individuals with the same competence profile.

Benefits

The process of scoring focuses on performance and competencies. It is relatively straightforward if the 360-degree data is available.

Limitations

The process relies on 360-degree feedback although it could conceivably be based on performance management ratings. It does not penetrate into measurements of the value as deeply as other methods.

EXAMPLES OF APPROACHES TO MEASUREMENT

The following examples are reported more fully in the reports from the CIPD Human Capital Panel (CIPD, 2006a, 2006b).

The Nationwide Building Society

The Nationwide Building Society feeds its human capital information into an intranet-based information system which gives users an assessment of how they are doing against a number of indicators. It uses a dashboard of red, amber and green indicators to give each business unit an idea of how the unit is faring on a number of key drivers of employee commitment (illustrated in Figure 6.4 in Chapter 6). This is backed up with advice on how improvements might be made.

Norwich Union Insurance

Norwich Union Insurance also feeds data into a dashboard, but the company additionally analyses the data to measure progress and impact on strategic activities and as a predictive tool to calculate outcomes from various possible actions.

The Royal Bank of Scotland

The Royal Bank of Scotland launched its human capital toolkit early in 2006. This gives all HR staff access to a wide range of key HR data methodologies and tools. The aim of the toolkit is to enable staff to align more closely the service they offer with the needs of the business. The information on offer enables staff to design and implement action plans with tangible bottom-line benefits. The introduction to the toolkit on the homepage states: 'the toolkit helps you in the diagnosis of issues within your business and is particularly valuable in the scoping of projects, in building business cases and comparing performance on people measures'.

The toolkit is divided into five work streams:

▌ surveys;

▌ measurement;

▌ research;

▌ benchmarking;

▌ reporting.

The surveys section gives staff access to a wide range of data and enables them to make internal comparisons between, for example, different call centres, as well as helping them understand how the figures relate to data on engagement or management effectiveness.

The human capital measures give staff access to a range of people and business metrics across the organization to show how the group's human capital model works. It lets them identify where improvements have been made and compare the performance of their business by means of a traffic-light system to see what further improvements are possible.

The research section brings together a range of facts on legislation, training and organizational development, as well as human capital facts like headcount, absence, turnover, etc. There is also tailored benchmarking that enables them to identify appropriate competitors to benchmark their performance against. Finally, staff have access to indexed human capital reports that have been published both internally and externally, together with current hot topics across the group.

Standard Chartered Bank

Standard Chartered Bank uses a human capital scorecard to analyse its data. This is produced on a quarterly and annual basis with various cuts of the same data produced for different business segments and countries, in addition to a global report. This comprises a series of slides with commentary to enable managers to understand the data.

The data is also included in twice-yearly board reviews on people strategy and forms part of the annual strategy planning process. The scorecard data is reviewed within each global business by a top team 'People Forum'. At country level, each local chief executive and his or her management committee reviews key trends in order to specify areas he or she needs to focus on.

In addition, Standard Chartered Bank uses qualitative analysis to examine trends and this has led the organization to identify the role of the manager as mediating the relationship between engagement and performance. In turn, this has led to a focus on qualitative research to identify what raises the bank's best managers above the rest. A further example is a qualitative analysis of high performance in selected customer-facing roles to determine which key behaviours continue to drive customer loyalty.

CONCLUSIONS

This chapter has reviewed the various measures of human capital that have been developed and are in use by a variety of organizations. It has also reviewed a number of analytical models and the relevance to human capital evaluation. It demonstrates that there are various levels of measurement. Basic measures give a snapshot picture of the workforce or current practice and if collected over time can identify trends or anomalies. There are also more sophisticated measures that can be used to established correlations and drive action or, at the highest level, measure the strategic capability of the organization.

6

Human capital reporting

Once we have generated information about human capital and its contribution to the business we must also be able to communicate this in a way that will have both relevance and value to a variety of stakeholders. Different stakeholders will require different kinds of information. For potential employees the issue will be about how much the company invests in their development and opportunities for them to progress. For customers it might be whether it engages in ethical practices with regard to workers or the environment. Potential suppliers will be interested in the nature of the relationship they can develop and how sustainable this will be over time, and investors will be interested in whether the firm has the resources required to increase profitability.

Although human capital is increasingly recognized as an important ingredient in business performance, it poses a distinctive set of problems for company reporting. As mentioned previously, unlike other assets of the firm, human capital is not owned by the organization, but is secured through the employment relationship.

In reporting terms, the implications of these features are that human capital cannot be readily incorporated in the financial statements of the firm. The Accounting for People Task Force, which examined the issue of external reporting and published its findings in 2003, concluded that external human capital data should be included in the Financial and Operating Review of companies (OFR).

However, when the Chancellor of the Exchequer announced that the OFR would be abolished in November 2005 external business reporting attracted a great deal of discussion. The subsequent development and consultation on the introduction of the Business Review as part of the EU Accounts Modernisation Directive has absorbed the requirements of the OFR and has extended business reporting to a wider range of organizations.

But good external reporting on human capital will only be possible if good quality internal data can been successfully generated and reported. The Accounting for People Task Force concluded:

> ... the way organizations manage their people affects their performance, Human Capital Management (HCM) – an approach to people management that treats it as a high level strategic issue and seeks systematically to analyse, measure and evaluate how people policies and practices create value – is winning recognition as a way of creating long-term sustainable performance in an increasingly competitive world.

This chapter will therefore first look at internal reporting on human capital and then at external reporting.

INTERNAL REPORTING

Internal reporting is still the most common form of reporting. Despite the requirements of the OFR and now the Business Review, very few companies are providing anything other than headline data externally. However, internal reporting is becoming increasingly sophisticated as organizations recognize the benefits of disseminating better and more accurate data around their organizations. The benefits of internal reporting include:

▌ better-informed decision making by managers about what kind of actions or practices will improve their business results;

▌ increasing ability to recognize problems and act on them before they escalate;

▌ recognition for the HR function as a source of information;

▌ increased ability to demonstrate the effectiveness of HR solutions and hence improve the argument for greater investment in HR practice.

The CIPD produced a guide on human capital reporting in 2004. This guide stresses that human capital evaluation and reporting is a journey. It does not matter where organizations join the road so long as they are all heading in the same direction with the aim of providing better-quality and more reliable information. The journey was described in Chapter 3 (see Figure 3.3) and moves from establishing the effectiveness of HR through demonstrating the contribution of process to human capital evaluation, measurement and management. Like all journeys you have to complete one stage before you can move on successfully to another and some organizations will have different starting points because of the information and capabilities already available to them.

The information resulting from the various stages on this journey is usually reported internally in the form of management reports providing information for line managers. However, this information will not be valued by line managers unless:

▌ It is credible, accurate and trustworthy.

▌ They understand what it means for them personally and how they manage their team.

▌ It is accompanied by guidance as to what action should be taken.

▌ They have the skills and abilities to understand and act upon it.

It is not enough simply to give managers and other stakeholders information on human capital. The information must be accompanied by effective analysis and explanation if they are going to understand and act upon it in the interests of maximizing organizational performance.

The evidence presented by Nalbantian *et al* (2004) indicates that there are three core principles behind effective HCM:

▌ Insist on systems thinking.

▌ Get the 'right' facts.

▌ Focus on value.

The first principle refers to getting a holistic approach to the development of processes. Business models and human capital strategies must match because they are interdependent. If elements of people management are developed in isolation without regard for other related activities, for example if a performance management system is developed without reference to training, they will almost certainly fail.

The second principle is about getting the right information and facts. This means seeing beyond the prevailing rhetoric and being prepared to probe and question attitudes and perceptions. Only facts will provide a firm basis for action. So it is no good continuing to claim that the organization pays for performance when the facts clearly demonstrate remuneration is dependent on length of service, or claiming to value people when the facts show there is no effort to evaluate their contribution to business.

The third principle is about focusing on value. For too long, line managers and executives have viewed people management as a variable cost that should be kept as low as possible. Human capital emphasizes that people should be viewed as value-generating assets. Through the measurement and analysis techniques discussed in the preceding chapters it is possible for organizations to identify the human capital drivers of productivity, service and performance. These drivers can both create and destroy value. Disciplined measurement of the actual drivers of performance in an organization can help prioritize interventions and improve the return on human capital investments.

The CIPD started research in this area of human capital evaluation and reporting back in 2000. In 2002 the Institute published the results of a piece of research commissioned from Scarborough and Elias from Warwick University showing that a virtuous circle (Figure 6.2) is generated by organizations committed to effective HCM.

Research by the Chartered Institute of Management (CIM) in 2006 demonstrates that a majority of organizations value their employees as key assets and believe that the activity of measuring and continuously developing and refining the understanding of human capital and its links to business performance is important. By linking management to measures, measures to reporting and reporting to management, some companies are beginning to build the credibility, information flows and knowledge necessary to embed a human capital perspective in management and measurement practices both at HR and top management level, and the level of belief that the CIM found will undoubtedly accelerate this process.

The basic model of human capital evaluation and reporting might therefore look something like Figure 6.2 opposite.

If this data collection cycle is completed properly the quality of the data and its analysis should improve over time and be tailored to the

Source: CIPD (2003)

Figure 6.1　The virtuous human capital circle

demands and needs of the recipients. In turn if recipients find the data helpful and trustworthy they are likely to demand more and more information, creating a virtuous cycle of data collection, analysis and reporting.

Human capital information will only bring about change if the recipients of the data value it, trust it and are prepared to allow it to inform their actions. Those actions might be whether or not to work

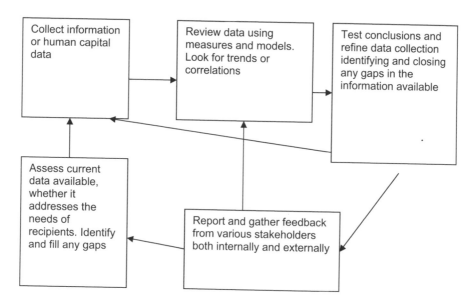

Figure 6.2　Evaluating and reporting on human capital

for the company, to invest in the company, to buy from the company or to supply to the company.

As a result there are various kinds of reporting the company needs to engage in to communicate effectively the relevant information on human capital to a range of audiences. This will include reporting both internally and externally.

Increasingly, organizations are using dashboards to communicate human capital information to line managers for information and decision-making purposes. The Nationwide Building Society has a sophisticated system based on their Genome II model (reported in CIPD, 2004). The model, which is based on the service–profit chain, has enabled them to make correlations between employee retention, customer satisfaction and commitment and business performance.

Through their use of dashboard information branch managers can assess their performance against a variety of indicators using a simple traffic light system and have access to guidance on remedial action if the dashboard indicates that they are not performing in particular areas.

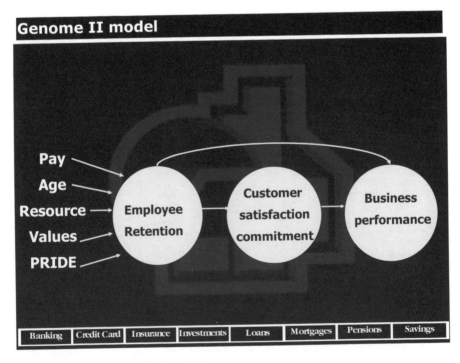

Source: The Nationwide Building Society

Figure 6.3   The Nationwide Building Society's Genome II model

Area	Key drivers of committed employees					Outcomes	
	Pay	Length of service	Coaching	Resource management	Values	Retention	Customer commitment
1	🟢	🟢	🟠	🟢	🟠	🟢	🟢
2	🟢	🟢	🟠	🟢	🟢	🟠	🟢
3	🟠	🟢	🟠	🟠	🔴	🟢	🟠
4	🟢	🟠	🔴	🟠	🟠	🟠	🟠
5	🔴	🟠	🟠	🔴	🔴	🔴	🔴

Green   Amber   Red

Figure 6.4 Human capital reporting dashboard for area managers: the Nationwide Building Society

EXTERNAL REPORTING

Much of the interest surrounding human capital in the last few years has been driven by the demands of investors, financial analysts and other stakeholders for better and more reliable data on long-term sustainable performance. As a result there has been a history of legislation. On 1 April 2005 the government introduced the mandatory Operating and Financial Review (OFR) for quoted companies in Great Britain (with the temporary exclusion of Northern Ireland).

This required all companies to provide in their annual reports a narrative report consisting of a balanced and comprehensive analysis, consistent with the size and complexity of the business of:

▌ the development and performance of the business during the financial year;

▌ the position of the company at the end of the year;

▌ the main trends and factors underlying the development, performance and position of the business of the company during the financial year;

▌ the main trends and factors likely to affect the company's future development, performance and position.

This had to be presented in such as way to enable the company's strategies to be assessed along with their potential to succeed. The OFR therefore had to include:

▌ a statement of the business, objectives and strategies of the business;

▌ a description of the resources available to the company;

▌ a description of the principal risks and uncertainties facing the company;

▌ a description of the capital structure, treasury policies and objectives and the liquidity of the company.

To comply with these requirements companies were advised to include information about the environment, employees, social and community issues plus the company's policies and how these have been implemented and to state which areas they were not including information on. They also had to include analysis using financial and where appropriate key performance indicators, including information in environment and employee matters.

However, in November 2005 the Chancellor of the Exchequer, Gordon Brown, abolished the OFR as a move to cut down on the bureaucracy faced by companies. This decision was greeted with astonishment from all sides, including the financial community, which had become increasingly aware that certain factors that most affected company valuations, including intangible value, were inadequately reported in company accounts and had seen the mandatory OFR as a significant improvement in increasing corporate transparency.

The result was a period of uncertainty. Many companies had already invested considerable time and effort in generating the information for an OFR. However, it quickly became apparent that underlying the decision to abolish the OFR was the realization that the EU Accounts Modernisation Directive replicated many of the provisions of the mandatory OFR by requiring companies to prepare a Business Review. This also applied to a far greater number of companies. Whereas the OFR had covered only quoted companies – amounting to less than 2,000 – the Business Review applies to around 40,000 companies excluding only those deemed as small under the accompanying definition.

The Business Review also requires companies to disclose information that is necessary for the understanding of the development, performance or position of the business of the company, including analysis using financial key performance indicators and, where appropriate, analysis using other key performance indicators. It also specifically requires inclusion of the main trends and factors likely to affect the future development performance and position of the company's business, and information about:

- environmental matters;

- employees;

- social and community issues.

Companies must include any information about any policies of the company in relation to these matters and their effectiveness.

The Minister for Industry and the Regions on announcing the changes to company law on 3 May 2006 said: 'Our aim has always been to encourage meaningful, strategic, forward-looking information to assist shareholder engagement while avoiding disproportionate burdens on business, in line with our better regulation agenda.'

In the CIPD's response to the Department of Trade and Industry's consultation on the Business Review, Duncan Brown, Assistant Director stated:

> We very much support the Government's desire to see a significant enhancement in the quantity and quality of narrative reporting on strategic, non-financial issues. But we believe that this will not be achieved without attending to the three key issues that we highlight in this response, which we feel have not been given due attention in the prior exercises, and despite the emphasis placed on them in the report of the government-established Accounting for People Task Force report.

The three issues referred to are:

∎ single area for narrative reporting;

∎ a requirement for reporting on human capital;

∎ guidance and support in reporting on human capital.

This summed up the frustration felt by the HR profession not only by erratic policy on the vehicle for business reporting but also the failure to implement the findings of the Accounting for People report in the OFR requirement. The Accounting for People Task Force clearly set out the importance and nature of reporting on human capital and yet in both the OFR legislation and in the Accounting Standards Board's guidance on its implementation there was no mention of human capital at all. The issue of materiality which had been stressed by Accounting for People and dropped from the OFR has been reinstated in the Business Review. However, it is still left largely to the discretion of directors whether or not they report on the performance and management of their people.

The current situation with regard to external business reporting on human capital has done nothing to encourage organizations to make anything other that headline statements on their human capital. This has done little to fulfil the demand for better information by the investment community. The Chartered Management Institute research concluded that among investors there appears to be a self-fulfilling prophecy. The researchers found that investors do not take much account of workforce metrics because there is little or no evidence of comparability, consistency or predictability in their presentation. However, they also found that the investors they interviewed believed that if HCM metrics were delivered on a dependable basis, they would be valuable when assessing organizational performance.

More work is needed to determine exactly what human capital information is needed, and more particularly what information HR needs to provide, to satisfy the demands of investors. However, in its guidance for members the CIPD has suggested a framework for external reporting (CIPD, 2003).

It is argued above that human capital cannot be treated in the same way as other forms of capital when it comes to measurement and reporting. However, human capital does still represent one of the most important predictors of business performance. The firm's ability to support its business strategy with human capital is an important indication of future business performance. It follows that the reporting of human capital should have a future orientation and that it embraces both historical data such as absence, headcount and pay, but also information about the development of future capabilities (training and development, workforce diversity and equality of opportunity).

Human capital is multi-dimensional and therefore a range of metrics will be required to adequately describe its character and contribution. Also, as pointed out above, because human capital is largely context dependent, different measures will have relevance for different organizations. The CIPD framework therefore suggests a number of dimensions on which reporting might take place with a range of potential measures for each. This is reflected in the following principles on which the framework is based:

- Firms *acquire and retain* human capital via the employment relationship – skills are mobile.

- Employee competencies are *developed* both through training and
  learning by doing.

- To add value, employee skills need to be *managed* – that is, motivated
  and applied to appropriate tasks.

- Human capital makes a significant contribution to corporate
  performance.

In other words, because of its dynamic nature, HCM demands multiple indicators. The CIPD argue:

Thus, rather than viewing human capital as a stable stock of skills, it may be more useful to view its value as resulting from the firm-level fit achieved between the flow of human resources and shifting market demands. In this view, an informed future-oriented assessment is concerned not only with *what* questions to do with the workforce skill-set etc. but also with *how* questions concerning the matching of such skills with business needs.

The CIPD goes on to say that these observations suggest that single-point measures of human capital are unhelpful or misleading on their own. For example, reporting human capital simply in terms of costs rather than value creation may result in cost reduction strategies rather than more desirable value creation activities.

The CIPD external reporting framework

The CIPD external reporting framework proposes a balanced scorecard approach to human capital encompassing indicators on a whole range of activities and measures. These are summarized in Figure 6.5.

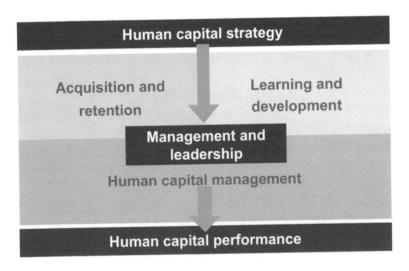

Figure 6.5 CIPD external reporting framework

The framework is based on the five categories of human capital strategy, acquisition and retention, development, management and performance. It proposes that each category includes a narrative describing how the firm is addressing the issues it contains plus a menu of key and discretionary indicators describing what outcomes are being achieved in relation to these activities.

Table 6.1 Principles of external reporting

Principle	Features of framework
Add value to the decision making undertaken by stakeholder groups in respect of human capital, with value added exceeding the costs of information gathered.	Information should be relevant to the identification of human capital and should be available in both narrative form and as quantitative indicators. The information-gathering requirement should be clearly defined and should not be too costly.
Balance the advantages of comparability with other organizations with the need for flexibility to reflect particular contexts.	There should be a distinction between primary and secondary indicators.
Provide information on possible institutional barriers to the effective development and utilization of human capital within firms.	Indicators to highlight possible barriers to the under-utilization of human capital based on gender, age or race.
Reflect the dynamic and context-dependent nature of human capital.	There should be multiple categories of indicators to reflect the acquisition, development, management and performance of human capital.
Be future-oriented to highlight the contribution of human capital to future performance.	The framework should incorporate information on both the near-term and the long-term situation, highlighting both investments in and depreciation of human capital. It should provide information not only on human capital stocks but also on the management and utilization of the flow of human capital.

The principles of reporting that this framework addresses are summarized in Table 6.1.

Human capital strategy

Reporting on human capital should begin with an account of the firm's human capital strategy. This would highlight the firm's overall approach to the acquisition, development, management and performance of human capital. The strategy statement allows the firm to outline its vision for the contribution of human capital in relation to future opportunities and challenges, and to outline the role of its HR policies in securing that contribution. It should be 'full and fair' so that the same level of top management responsibility for its accuracy and relevance is attached to it as for other, more traditional areas of reporting.

Sections on acquisition and retention, development and management

The report on human capital strategy should be supported by evidence on how the organization acquires, develops, manages and retains human capital. The evidence organizations are able to provide and what is appropriate will depend on their individual circumstances. The evidence should be a balance of both quantitative and qualitative data. Quantitative data in particular can be misleading and therefore adequate explanation will be required.

Information on performance

Finally, organizations should provide details of the effectiveness and performance of their human capital and HCM policies and practices again using a mix of quantitative and qualitative data to indicate how effectively their strategic objectives are being achieved.

Further details are provided below of what this framework might look like, together with guidance and examples of the types of data that could be included in the reporting process to give a balanced account of human capital. It is proposed that each section should include a narrative of key indicators explaining the organization's approach to the area of activity, any difficulties it needs to overcome that are specific to its operating circumstances, location or industry, and the strategy for the development of policy. There follows two sets of indicators: primary indicators that could be indicative of the investment and return on human capital in all or most circumstances, and secondary indicators which might be used to explain key data or might be indicative of particular operating and environmental circumstances.

Under each of the categories a distinct section on management and leadership is proposed. The importance of the leadership population of the organization was highlighted by the consultation undertaken by the CIPD. It was felt that information on human capital utilization for this category of employees, which has the greatest scope to impact on the strategic performance of the organization, will be most readily available and has particular value to financial analysts and investors. This is evidenced by the fact that the remuneration of company directors is already an important component of annual reports.

Details of the framework under the headings of a narrative and a list of primary and secondary indicators for the activity areas (each of which includes management and leadership in recognition of its significance) is set out as Table 6.2.

Table 6.2 External reporting framework

Activity area	Narrative – near-term and long-term	Primary indicators	Secondary Indicators
Acquisition and retention	How the firm sources its supply of human capital; composition of the workforce in terms of diversity and employment relationships (full-time, temporary, etc) Policies for the retention of key skills	Average number of vacancies as a percentage of the total workforce per month/year Ratio of internal to external recruitment for job vacancies Salaries and benefits costs – breakdown by full-time and temporary worker costs Average length of time taken to fill vacancies Staff turnover – averages for different levels of management and employees	Composition of the workforce in terms of age, gender or race Costs of recruitment Length of service distribution (eg percentage less than 2 years, percentage less than 10, percentage less than 20) Return on human capital (profits/payroll and training costs) Evidence of skills shortage or shortfall of skill between what is required and that possessed by job applicants
Management and leadership	How the firm sources a supply of leadership talent Succession planning practices and category and number of the organizational population they cover Size of the relevant talent pool Remuneration policies	Composition of board and executive team – age, gender, experience. Percentage of variable pay at senior levels Percentage of senior managers recruited internally/externally	Turnover in senior management, percentage per annum Performance criteria for senior management and extent to which this links to remuneration

Table 6.2 External reporting framework *(continued)*

Activity area	Narrative – near-term and long-term	Primary indicators	Secondary Indicators
Learning and development	How the firm develops its human capital. Training and development policy. Skills levels of the workforce. Development strategy in terms of raising skills levels, changing the skills mix. Strategy for the provision of training. Aims and objectives of training and development	Off-the-job training days/FTE as percentages by category and grade of staff Expenditure on off-the-job training (overall and as percentages by categories and grade of staff) Expenditure on workplace learning (overall and as percentages by categories and grade of staff)	Number of employees who have attained a particular competency level Number of employees attaining formal qualifications, including NVQs Number of internal promotions Number of employees who complete personal development plans Expenditure on career counselling/planning
Management and leadership	Approach to management development and details of management development programmes. Criteria used to determine management competence	Management development spend per manager Average number of days training per year per manager	Number of managers possessing formal management qualifications Length of time required for managers to attain satisfactory level of competence Staff or customer data on management ability
Human capital management	How the firm manages (motivates and aligns) its human capital Expressed values of the organization with regard to the preferred management style Management policy and practice on selection, communication, consultation, appraisal and reward, and human capital evaluation. Operation of consultation and involvement schemes, Works Council arrangements, trade union structure Structure and delivery of HR services	HR spend per employee Percentage of employees covered by formal HR policies in the following areas ● recruitment and selection ● training and development ● appraisal and performance management ● job design ● communication, consultation and employee involvement ● financial flexibility (performance/team-based rewards) ● harmonization ● employment security	Available benchmark indicators based on recognized methodology/standard Measures of employee commitment Measures of employee satisfaction Percentage of shares held by employees Percentage of variable pay by category and grade of employee Percentage of employees covered by company share schemes

Activity area	Narrative – near-term and long-term	Primary indicators	Secondary Indicators
Management and leadership	Induction programme for directors Criteria used to determine leadership potential	Days per year spent resourcing top team development	
Performance	The value created by human capital. Indications of the strategy for the collection and retention of knowledge. Criteria used to determine individual and team performance	Market capitalization per employee Revenue per employee Profit per employee Sales per employee	Adjusted profit/ employee Unit productivity/ employee Measures of customer satisfaction Measures of employee satisfaction and loyalty
Management and leadership	Value created by management and leadership. Development of firm capabilities. Durability of management strategy	Percentage flow of human capital in and out of the organization	Employee perceptions of management

CONCLUSIONS

This chapter has summarized the issues surrounding both internal and external reporting and argued that any human capital information has first to be credible and reliable so that the recipients can trust it. The information must also be accompanied by adequate explanation and analysis to enable recipients to understand what it means for them. It must be linked to action with appropriate guidance and support and it must be multi-dimensional, reflecting the unique character of human capital.

7

Applications of HCM

HCM is an integral part of the people management process – it does not lead a separate existence. It illuminates, guides and supports the key HRM activities discussed in this chapter, namely strategic HRM, talent management, learning and development, knowledge management, performance management, reward management and the support and development of line managers.

HCM data can be used to evaluate the impact of HR strategies and to identify areas in which they could add most value. It can provide information on causation – how results are affected by HR policies and actions. But it is notoriously difficult to establish causation when investigating the relationship between an HR initiative and an outcome. There are too many other factors that get in the way, ie multi-causation. Attempts can be made to allow for the influence of other variables but they can often only be made on the basis of questionable assumptions.

THE LINK BETWEEN HCM AND STRATEGIC HRM

HCM provides the basis for strategic HRM through measurement and analysis leading to evaluation, diagnosis and action. As Kearns (2006) contends, 'HCM is only concerned with outputs, results and value – right from the outset – and designs its interventions and activities accordingly.'

Walker (1992) defines strategic HRM as 'the means of aligning the management of human resources with the strategic content of the business'. It can be described as an approach to making decisions on the intentions and plans of the organization in the shape of the policies, programmes and practices concerning the employment relationship, talent management, knowledge management, learning and development, performance management, reward, and employee relations. The concept of strategic HRM is derived from the concepts of HRM and strategy. It takes the HRM model with its focus on strategy, integration and coherence and adds to that the key notion of resource-based strategy. The link between HCM and resource-based theory is that both emphasize the importance of human capital as a means of adding value and both recognize the importance of strategic planning that is based on an understanding of the factors that have a direct impact of the performance of people in the organization.

A resource-based approach to strategic HRM focuses on satisfying the human capital requirements of the organization by reference to the data provided by human capital measurements. The notion of resource-based strategic HRM is based on the ideas of Penrose (1959) who wrote that the firm is 'an administrative organization and a collection of productive resources'. The approach was developed by Hamel and Prahalad (1989) who declared that competitive advantage is obtained if a firm can obtain and develop human resources that enable it to learn faster and apply its learning more effectively than its rivals. Barney (1991) states that sustained competitive advantage stems from the acquisition and effective use of bundles of distinctive resources that competitors cannot imitate. As Purcell et al (2003) suggest, the values and HR policies of an organization constitute an important non-imitable resource. This is achieved by ensuring that (1) the firm has higher-quality people than its competitors; (2) the unique intellectual capital possessed by the business is developed and nurtured; (3) organizational learning is encouraged; (4) organization-specific values and a culture exist which 'bind the organization together (and) gives it focus'. Resource-based theory is linked to human capital theory; they both emphasize that investment in people adds to their value to the firm.

HCM indicates the direction to be taken by a resource-based approach in order to improve resource capability – achieving strategic fit between resources and opportunities and obtaining added value from the effective deployment of human capital. Resource-based strategy, as

Barney (1991) indicates, can develop strategic capability and produce what Boxall (1996) refers to as human resource advantage.

A strategic HCM approach involves identifying the drivers of organizational performance such as customer service, innovation, quality and sales/cost leadership. The key attributes people need to deliver effective performance can then be identified and defined in terms of recruitment and promotion specifications, skills, competencies and upholding corporate values. The degree to which individuals have the required attributes can be included in performance review processes. A direct link can be made, as at the NSPCC, between evolving corporate strategies and values so that as these are redefined, they can specifically become part of the performance planning and review process. At Selfridges, as reported by Purcell *et al* (2003), a key element of the business strategy was to enhance and promote the Selfridges brand. As a result conscious steps were taken to improve the brand image among both Selfridges staff and staff employed in the various concessionary retail outlets on the shop floor. An assessment tool was developed based on the competencies and behaviours that were found to be most positive in promoting customer care and the external brand they were keen to foster. This was used in both recruitment and promotion to ensure that those appointed had the behavioural characteristics required by the company as well as the necessary skills.

Taking this one step further there were several examples among the companies interviewed for this book where the HR function was actively developing human capital measures aligned to the business strategy. Centrica (CIPD, 2006a), for example, took the business strategy as its starting point and then identified what the organization would have to measure to monitor progress against that strategy.

Becker *et al* (2001) refer to the need to develop a 'high-performance perspective' in which HR and other executives view HR as a system embedded within the larger system of the firm's strategy implementation. They state that: 'The firm manages and measures the relationship between these two systems and firm performance.' A high-performance work system is a crucial part of this approach in that it:

▌ links the firm's selection and promotion decisions to validated competency models;

▌ develops strategies that provide timely and effective support for the skills demanded by the firm's strategy implementation;

▌ enacts compensation and performance management policies that attract, retain and motivate high-performance employees.

Lloyds TSB has produced the following definition of what they mean by a high-performance organization as part of their HCM programme:

▌ People know what's expected of them – they are clear about their goals and accountabilities.

▌ They have the skills and competencies to achieve their goals.

▌ High performance is recognized and rewarded accordingly.

▌ People feel that their job is worth doing, and that there's a strong fit between the job and their capabilities.

▌ Managers act as supportive leaders and coaches, providing regular feedback, performance reviews and development.

▌ A pool of talent ensures a continuous supply of high performers in key roles.

▌ There is a climate of trust and teamwork, aimed at delivering a distinctive service to the customer.

HCM AND TALENT MANAGEMENT

Kearns (2006) sees HCM as being about having 'fully competent, fully informed employees who are in a position to make critical decisions in a flexible but well-controlled organization'. HCM is thus at the heart of talent management.

The aim of talent management is to secure the flow of talent, bearing in mind that talent is a major corporate resource. It can refer simply to management succession planning and management development activities and this notion does not really add anything to these familiar processes except a new, although admittedly more evocative, name. Talent management can also be regarded as a more comprehensive and integrated set of activities to ensure that the organization attracts, retains, motivates and develops the talented people it needs now and in the future. As stated by Saratoga (2005): 'The key ingredients of a disciplined talent management system [are] the identification, attraction, retention, development and usage of talent.'

It is often assumed that talent management is only concerned with key people – the high flyers. For example, Smilansky (2005) states that it is 'aimed at improving the calibre, availability and flexible utilisation of exceptionally capable (high potential) employees who can have a disproportionate impact on business performance'. But it can be argued that everyone in an organization has talent even if some have more talent than others and that talent management processes should not be limited to the favoured few. This point was made by deLong and Vijayaraghavan (2003) when they suggested that the unsung heroes of corporate performance are the capable, steady performers.

The elements of talent management

The elements of talent management as a comprehensive approach and their interrelationships are shown in Figure 7.1.

The areas of measurement and action are set out in Table 7.1.

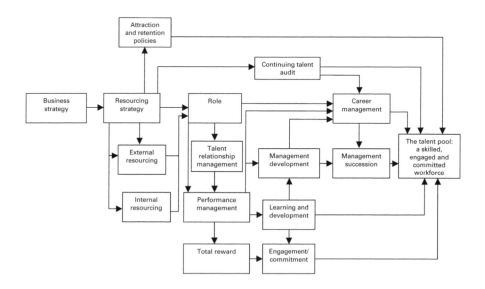

Figure 7.1 Elements of talent management

Table 7.1 Talent management: human capital measures and actions

Area	Measures	Possible actions
Attrition	<ul><li>Index of employee turnover</li><li>Survival rates</li><li>Half-life index</li><li>Stability index</li><li>Length of service analysis</li></ul>	<ul><li>Improve recruitment and selection processes</li><li>Make 'employer of choice' plans</li><li>Provide better remuneration packages (more competitive and equitable)</li><li>Carry out risk analysis (potential leavers)</li><li>Deal with induction crisis</li></ul>
Cost of employee turnover	<ul><li>Leaving costs</li><li>Direct replacement costs (advertising, interviewing, testing, etc)</li><li>Direct cost of induction for replacements</li><li>Direct cost of training replacements</li><li>Opportunity cost of time spent by HR and line managers in recruitment and induction</li><li>Loss of input/contribution from those who have left before they are replaced</li><li>Loss arising from reduced input/contribution from new starters until they reach the required level of competence as displayed by fully trained and experienced employees</li></ul>	<ul><li>Use cost of employee turnover data to support the business case for actions such as those listed above against attrition, eg by spelling out how much money would be saved by taking particular actions and therefore the impact on the bottom line</li></ul>
Performance and potential	<ul><li>Assessments of performance and potential obtained through performance management processes</li></ul>	<ul><li>Introduce/improve general learning and development programmes to improve performance</li><li>Provide focused individual learning programmes dealing with performance issues or developing competencies for the future</li></ul>
Management succession	<ul><li>Analysis of data on who is available to succeed individuals in key jobs and to identify gaps</li></ul>	<ul><li>Launch external recruitment programmes to obtain people with potential</li><li>Carry out internal 'trawls' to identify people with potential</li></ul>
HR planning	<ul><li>Analysis of data on who is available to succeed individuals in key jobs to identify gaps</li></ul>	<ul><li>Plan recruitment</li><li>Devise training programmes</li></ul>
Evaluation of learning and development programmes	<ul><li>ROI calculations</li><li>Impact assessments (individual and collective)</li></ul>	<ul><li>Justify programmes</li><li>Improve programmes</li></ul>

HCM AND LEARNING AND DEVELOPMENT

HCM is based on the conviction that people are assets and investing in them will create added value. The major vehicles for such investments are learning and development programmes. To apply HCM techniques it is first necessary to appreciate the nature of learning and development and then to understand methods of evaluation as a means of developing data that can be used to justify and plan learning and development programmes.

The nature of learning and development

Learning is a continuous process that not only enhances existing capabilities but also leads to the development of the skills, knowledge and attitudes that prepare people for enlarged or higher level responsibilities in the future.

The encouragement of learning makes use of a process model concerned with facilitating the learning activities of individuals and providing learning resources for them to use. Conversely, the provision of training involves the use of a content model which means deciding in advance the knowledge and skills that need to be enhanced by training, planning the programme, deciding on training methods and presenting the content in a logical sequence through various forms of instruction. Today the approach is to focus on individual learning and ensure that it takes place when required – ' just-for-you' and 'just-in-time' learning.

Watkins and Marsick (1993) defined a spectrum of learning from informal to formal experiences as:

▌ unanticipated experiences and encounters that result in learning as an incidental by-product, which may or may not be consciously recognized;

▌ new job assignments and participation in teams, or other job-related challenges that provide for learning and self-development;

▌ self-initiated and self-planned experiences, including the use of media and seeking out a coach or mentor;

▌ total quality or improvement groups/active learning designed to promote continuous learning for continuous improvement;

▌ providing a framework for learning associated with personal development planning or career planning;

▌ the combination of less-structured with structured opportunity to learn from these experiences;

▌ designed programmes of mentoring, coaching or workplace learning;

▌ formal training programmes or courses involving instruction.

Learning programmes are concerned with:

▌ defining the objectives of learning;

▌ creating an environment in which effective learning can take place (a learning culture);

▌ adopting a systematic, planned and balanced approach to the delivery of learning;

▌ identifying learning and development needs;

▌ satisfying these needs by making use of blended learning approaches – eg self-managed learning, e-learning and training;

▌ evaluating the effectiveness of these processes.

Measures of the impact and effectiveness of training

The three methods of measuring training are training evaluation, return on investment (ROI) and quantitative data as described below.

Training evaluation

Four levels of training evaluation have been suggested by Kirkpatrick (1994):

Level 1. Reaction – at this level, evaluation measures how those who participated in the training have reacted to it. In a sense, it is a measure of immediate customer satisfaction.

Level 2. Evaluating learning – this level obtains information on the extent to which learning objectives have been attained. It will aim to find how much knowledge was acquired, what skills were developed or improved, and, as appropriate, the extent to which attitudes have changed in the desired direction. So far as possible, the evaluation of learning should involve the use of tests before and after the programme – paper and pencil or performance tests.

Level 3. Evaluating behaviour – this level evaluates the extent to which behaviour has changed as required when people attending the programme have returned to their jobs. The question to be answered is the extent to which knowledge, skills and attitudes have been transferred from the training to the workplace. Ideally, the evaluation should take place both before and after the training. Time should be allowed for the change in behaviour to take place. The evaluation needs to assess the extent to which specific learning objectives relating to changes in behaviour and the application of knowledge and skills have been achieved.

Level 4. Evaluating results – this is the ultimate level of evaluation and provides the basis for assessing the benefits of the training against its costs. The evaluation has to be based on before and after measures and has to determine the extent to which the fundamental objectives of the training have been achieved in areas such as increasing sales, raising productivity, reducing accidents or increasing customer satisfaction. Evaluating results is obviously easier when they can be quantified. However, it is not always easy to prove the contribution to improved results made by training as distinct from other factors and as Kirkpatrick says: 'Be satisfied with evidence, because proof is usually impossible to get.'

ROI

Some commentators believe that the best means of assessing the overall impact of training on organizational performance is the ROI it generates. ROI is calculated by the following formula:

$$\frac{\text{Benefits from training (£)} - \text{costs of training (£)} \times 100}{\text{Costs of training (£)}}$$

Kearns and Miller (1997) contend that only this sort of measure is useful in evaluating the overall impact of training. They argue that particular hard measures should be used to evaluate specific training;

for example, if development aims to bring about greater awareness of customers then it should be measured by the eventual effect on customer spend, customer satisfaction and number of customers.

The pressure to produce financial justifications for any organizational activity, especially in areas such as learning and development, has increased the interest in ROI. The problem is that while it is easy to record the costs it is much harder to produce convincing financial assessments of the benefits. Kearns (2005b) provides a response to this concern:

> All business is about the art of speculation and the risk of the unknown. The trick here is not to try and work to a higher standard of credibility than anyone else in the organization. If accountants are prepared to guess about amortisation costs or marketing directors to guess about market share why should a trainer not be prepared to have a guess at the potential benefits of training?

He recommends the use of 'a rule of thumb' when using ROI to the effect that any training should improve the performance of trainees by at least 1 per cent. Thus, if the return on sales training is being measured, the benefits could be calculated as 1 per cent of profit on sales.

Mayo (2004) suggests that there are two connected types of 'return' that can be used to judge whether an HR function is spending money and time to best advantage: the 'future value added' for stakeholders; the 'return on investment' from specific projects and programmes. These could apply to training or to any other activity.

Competency measurement

Another method of evaluation is to measure increases in levels of competency as established by performance management.

Quantitative data

Quantitative data that indicates activity levels includes:

▌ personal development plans completed as a percentage of employees;

▌ training hours per employee;

▌ percentage of managers taking part in formal development programmes.

But these measures give no indication of quality in terms of impact on performance and results.

KNOWLEDGE MANAGEMENT

Knowledge is a vital part of the human capital resources in a firm bearing in mind that human capital is an element of intellectual capital which consists of the stocks and flows of knowledge available to an organization. Knowledge management is 'any process or practice of creating, acquiring, capturing, sharing and using knowledge, wherever it resides, to enhance learning and performance in organizations' (Scarborough *et al*, 1999). These authors suggest that knowledge management focuses on the development of firm-specific knowledge and skills that are the result of organizational learning processes. Knowledge management is concerned with both stocks and flows of knowledge. Stocks include expertise and encoded knowledge in computer systems. Flows represent the ways in which knowledge is transferred from people to people or from people to a knowledge database. As explained by Blake (1988), the purpose of knowledge management is to capture a company's collective expertise and distribute it to 'wherever it can achieve the biggest payoff'.

Knowledge management is about storing and sharing the wisdom understanding and expertise accumulated in an organization about its processes, techniques and operations. It treats knowledge as a key resource. Ulrich (1998) points out that: 'Knowledge has become a direct competitive advantage for companies selling ideas and relationships.'

As a key component of intellectual capital, knowledge management is as much if not more concerned with people (human capital) and how they acquire, exchange and disseminate knowledge as it is about information technology. That is why it has become an important area for HR practitioners who are in a strong position to exert influence in this aspect of people management. Scarborough *et al* (1999) believe that they should have 'the ability to analyse the different types of knowledge deployed by the organization... [and] to relate such knowledge to issues of organizational design, career patterns and employment security.'

Research from the CIPD (Kinnie *et al*, 2006) investigates the key processes that link people management practices and organizational performance in professional service firms. It looks in particular at how HR contributes to the creation of tangible value in the form of knowledge-based outputs. For professional service firms the knowledge of their staff is the key to the development of intellectual capital. As one of the case study interviewees put it: 'We are a people business, what we sell are our people and the value they can add to clients.'

This research has found that if we really want to understand how HR contributes to the value creation process we need not only to evaluate and understand human capital but also the other forms of capital. These include:

- social or relational capital in the form of social, client and network capital defining the relationships between individual and groups in formal and informal settings;

- structural capital defining the physical work arrangements and the ability to leverage these for optimal knowledge conversion;

- production and organizational capital comprising the specific technologies, policies and procedures, including HR policies.

The research concludes that if firms can establish organizational capital that ensures faster, higher-quality and more cost-effective conversion of human capital into intellectual capital they are more likely to be able to establish a sustainable advantage over their competitors. Because organizational capital tends to be very firm-specific it is not easily transferable from one organization to another and hence a greater understanding of the relationships between all these forms of capital and how they interact to facilitate the conversion of knowledge into value can significantly inform the development of HR processes that will have an impact on business performance.

The research also demonstrates that particular HR policies will be of value to help build the different forms of capital and facilitate positive relationships between all forms of capital, which will enable knowledge to flow more freely and easily around the organization. In order to convert knowledge into organizational value there must be knowledge creation to develop new knowledge, knowledge transfer when knowledge owned by one individual or group is shared with another, and knowledge integration where new solutions of approaches become part of the organizational memory either through their integration into organizational routines or through their recording in systems and procedures used across the organization.

Knowledge management is therefore a key component of HCM and an essential component in the process of developing intellectual capital. As such, an HCM approach to knowledge management is about 'systematically and actively managing and leveraging the stores of knowledge in an organization' (Tan, 2000). It is not so much concerned with metrics except, possibly, records of activity levels, for example the achievements of communities of interests in sharing knowledge and ensuring that it is put to good use.

PERFORMANCE MANAGEMENT AS A SOURCE OF HUMAN CAPITAL DATA

Performance management processes provide an important source of information on human capital and its contribution to business. Lawler (2003) has made the point that: 'It is very difficult to effectively manage human capital without a system that measures performance and performance capability... An effective performance management system should be a key building block of every organization's human capital management system.'

At the very basic level the performance management process informs organizations how well individuals are achieving their objectives. Of the respondents to the CIPD 2003/04 survey 62 per cent were using objective setting as part of the performance management process and for the majority this meant objectives linked to the business strategy. The case study research conducted by Armstrong and Baron (2004) found that many performance management systems are designed to assess inputs to the performance process in terms of the skills and experience that people bring to the job as well as outputs in the forms of achievement of objectives. It was also established that more and more organizations are managing performance not just in terms of what people do but also how they do it. Behaviour frameworks are increasingly common and a number of systems have processes in place both to define and communicate appropriate levels of behaviour to individuals.

Use of performance management data

Performance management data is obtained from the outcomes of performance reviews and 360-degree assessments. It can inform on the levels of capability, readiness for promotion or job expansion, match between required and actual behaviour and competence levels. The data can provide insights on the value of human capital. More than a third of the respondents to the CIPD survey were assessing competence and/or feeding performance data into succession plans and career management.

Performance management data can be used to:

■ demonstrate an organization's ability to raise competence levels;

■ assess how long it takes for a new employee to reach optimum performance;

■ provide feedback on development programmes including induction, coaching and mentoring in terms of increased performance or capacity to take on new roles;

■ demonstrate the success of internal recruitment programmes;

■ indicate how successful an organization is at achieving its objectives at the individual, team and department level;

■ track skills levels and movement in any skills gap in the organization;

■ match actual behaviour against desired behaviour;

■ assess commitment to values and mission;

■ assess understanding of strategy and contribution.

Most of this information is already captured during performance management activities. To turn it into measure of human capital evaluation, the data needs to be processed in a more systematic and widely accessible way.

One organization that is well advanced in terms of human capital reporting is Norwich Union. Marie Sigsworth, Director of HR Customer Service, interviewed for the 2004 book on performance management published by the CIPD, said:

> We report against 101 different key performance indicators (KPIs) and obviously the thing that we are focusing on at the moment is how you make sure that they are the right ones. You could measure an awful lot so we need to decide what the key measures are that we need to be looking at.
>
> We have a dashboard which is the tool the team manager has for assisting planning and allocating work and capturing and graphically reporting on the

KPI data. So the team manager can sit there with his [or her] team and say look our customer service stats are right down, what are we doing as a team? How are we going to pull that round? It gives the manager real-time data to work with [the] team in their huddles, they see it and talk about what they can do.

There's also a productivity measure so the team managers can talk about it in a huddle at team level or pick it up as individuals in one to one's or coaching sessions.

The use of dashboards, as at Norwich Union, to make measures of the people contribution and information available to all managers on a daily basis is becoming more widespread. This has implications for how performance management is carried out and the requirements for managers to feed good-quality data into effective data management systems.

Evaluation of performance management

Both the 1997/98 and the 2003/04 CIPD surveys of performance management found little evidence that organizations were systematically evaluating the effectiveness of their performance management processes. Such evaluation is a fundamental characteristic of HCM and in the important area of performance management it is something that organizations ought to do as a matter of course. Performance management does not always work well and it is important to identify any weakness so that the performance of performance management can be improved.

One fairly crude indication used by some organizations is the percentage of people who have had a formal performance review. But this is purely a quantitative measure; there is no indication of the quality of the review meeting, which is what counts. This is where opinion surveys can produce useful data. An example of such a survey is given in the Appendix (see page 188). Another measure is the distribution of performance ratings by categories of staff and department. This can be used to indicate inconsistencies, questionable distributions and trends in assessments.

The ultimate test, of course, is analysing organizational performance to establish the extent to which improvements can be attributed to performance management. This requires measurements of the 'before or after' effect, ie corporate performance as it was before and after performance management was introduced. For existing performance management processes, the aim would be to link measures of the effectiveness of performance management with measures of corporate performance.

An attempt to prove a connection between performance management and business performances was made by McDonald and Smith (1991). They conducted research covering 437 publicly quoted US companies, 205 with performance management and 232 without. The findings were that the 205 respondents with performance management as opposed to the others demonstrated:

▌ higher profits, better cash flows, stronger stock market performance and higher stock value;

▌ significant gains over three years in financial performance and productivity;

▌ higher sales growth per employee;

▌ lower real growth in number of employees.

It is a matter of speculation as to whether the results in the most effective companies were created by performance management or whether the most effective companies were the ones most likely to introduce performance management. This is the reverse causation phenomenon.

Another attempt to measure the impact of performance management on corporate performance was made by Guest (then of Birkbeck College) and his colleagues using data on the effectiveness of performance management obtained by the IPD in 1997/98 (Armstrong and Baron, 1998). Multi-variant analysis was used, which revealed that the respondents rated performance management effectiveness very positively – over 90 per cent of them rated performance management as being moderately or highly effective.

But Guest raised a number of caveats. The Birkbeck analysis indicated that the views of respondents to the survey should all be viewed with extreme caution since they were often based on a very limited form of formal evaluation, or on an absence of any formal evaluation. This, said Guest, raises serious questions about the basis for the generally positive assessment of performance management. Further more detailed statistical analysis by Birkbeck of the replies to the questionnaire failed to demonstrate consistent evidence of any link between the practice of performance management and outcomes such as the achievement of financial targets, achievement of quality and customer service goals and employee development goals.

But this does not mean that an attempt to evaluate should not be made, especially if a comprehensive approach is used such as the one adopted by an NHS Trust (referred to in Armstrong and Baron, 2004) which involved:

▌ recording and analysing performance assessments to establish how managers are using performance management;

▌ one-to-one interviews with managers identifying how they are finding the experience of performance management and where they need more support;

▌ employee attitude surveys and focused discussion groups;

▌ reviewing improvements in the performance of the organization.

The outcome of this analysis provided the data required to carry out the following actions to maintain high standards:

▌ Continue training in performance management for all new staff (including individuals who are promoted to management posts).

▌ Top up training to keep the principles and practices fresh.

▌ Use one-to-one coaching where necessary.

▌ Conduct workshops for managers to share their experiences.

REWARD MANAGEMENT

Reward management deals with the design, implementation and maintenance of reward systems (reward processes, practices and procedures) that aim to meet the needs of both the organization and its stakeholders. Its aims are to:

▌ reward people according to what the organization values and wants to pay for;

▌ reward people for the value they create;

▌ achieve equity (especially the provision of equal pay for work of equal value), fairness and consistency in dealing with reward matters;

▌ reward the right things to convey the right message about what is important in terms of behaviours and outcomes;

▮ develop a performance culture;

▮ motivate people and obtain their commitment and engagement;

▮ help to attract and retain the high-quality people the organization needs.

An HCM approach to reward management will basically assemble data on remuneration, but in a more advanced form will attempt to assess the impact of remuneration policies on people and the business.

The basic measurements include the following:

▮ The effectiveness of the job evaluation scheme from the point of view of the extent to which it has decayed, how relevant it is to present working arrangements, the degree to which it provides the basis for fair and equitable grading decisions and for preventing grade drift and whether or not it is too bureaucratic or time consuming.

▮ Progress towards achieving equal pay for work of equal value using equal pay review procedures. These will establish the incidence of pay gaps between male and female workers and lead to an analysis of the cause of the gaps and decisions on how they can be remedied.

▮ The distribution of actual salaries to establish how pay practice (actual pay) compares with pay policy (the rate for a person who is fully qualified and competent in his or her job) by reference to compa-ratios that measure the relationship between actual and policy rates of pay as a percentage.

▮ The extent to which pay levels are competitive and contribute to the attraction and retention of high-quality staff.

▮ The incidence of attrition to pay costs that takes place when employees enter jobs at lower rates of pay than the previous job holders and the implications for pay policy (large attrition rates may reduce and therefore justify contingent pay costs).

▮ Analyses of the distribution of pay awards by managers to identify inconsistencies or a tendency not to differentiate rewards according to performance.

▮ The cost of the implementation of pay reviews against budget.

▮ Total payroll costs.

▋ Total pay review increases for different categories of employees as a percentage of pay.

▋ Average bonuses or contingent pay increases as a percentage of pay for different categories of employees.

Analysing the impact of reward policies presents the usual problems of selecting measures and establishing causation. Ideally measures are selected that define the action and the outcome and link them together, although they may be difficult to find, as was the case in the performance management study referred to above. Establishing causation can be difficult if there are a number of factors involved (multiple causation). It could, for example, be argued that better pay for customer service staff has led to increased customer satisfaction and more sales. But increased customer satisfaction could be contributed to by an improved and cheaper product and higher sales may be influenced by lower prices or increases in market share arising from marketing initiatives. Somehow, these other influences have to be discounted and this is very difficult except by making huge and often unsustainable assumptions.

Very occasionally it is possible to make accurate measurements without any significant distorting factors. An instance is provided in a large distribution centre with 400 staff where it was thought that productivity would be increased by a work-measured bonus scheme. An initial study by consultants found that the overall productivity rate for the centre was 90 compared with the norm of 100. The scheme was introduced and the results measured after a year and it was established that the productivity rate had gone up to 109. This meant improved levels of customer service and cost savings resulting from reduction in staff numbers by natural wastage.

Another approach to measuring the effectiveness of reward policies and practices is to conduct an attitude survey to measure the opinions of employees about the reward system. An example of a survey is given in the Appendix (see page 192).

SUPPORTING AND DEVELOPING LINE MANAGERS

One of the main conclusions reached from the research carried out by Hutchinson and Purcell into the role of frontline managers (2003) was that 'bringing policies to life and leading was among the most important factors in explaining the difference between success and mediocrity in people management'. HCM can help to support and develop line managers in this exacting role by providing them with information on how well they are doing as people managers in such areas as exercising leadership, productivity, improving customer service and controlling employee turnover and absenteeism.

Line managers can be provided with the outcome of surveys of leadership, engagement and commitment and customer views about service levels. Dashboards can be set up on the intranet which, as in the Nationwide Building Society, provide a traffic-light system for telling managers how they are doing under various headings. This is accompanied by suggested actions that the managers should take to improve their performance. The metrics are therefore useful as a tool for HR to encourage managers to take certain actions and to convince them of the value of implementing HR processes.

Many of the practitioners interviewed for this book stressed that metrics alone, while providing managers with information, would not necessarily be enough to drive performance. Indeed in some instances metrics may be the source of poor performance if they encourage the wrong behaviour. One manager gave a graphic example of this, explaining how managers were given the results of an attitude survey where respondents gave a generally negative view of the organization. They were told that improvements must be made but not how to do it, with the result that some told their employees to 'give the right answers or else!' Metrics must be supported by suggested action and explanation if they are going to result in better support and ultimately better management.

Possibly some of the best application of metrics arises when they are used as a basis for HR to provide managers with good-quality advice and guidance and as evidence of learning and development needs, collectively or individually.

Part 3

The role and future of HCM

8

The role of HR in HCM

As noted in Chapter 2, the whole area of HCM presents both an opportunity and a challenge for the HR profession. It is an opportunity because it provides a vehicle for demonstrating that people are adding value and for indicating ways in which value-adding behaviour can be encouraged. It can help to transform the rhetoric surrounding the concept of HR people as business partners into reality. It can enhance the contribution HR can make to shaping business strategy and enable the function to align its strategies to business and people needs. It is a challenge because it means that HR must adopt a business-oriented as well as a people-oriented approach to its work and it has to do this by processes of measurement and analysis which must be much more rigorous and focused than has typically been the case in the past.

HCM is a business-oriented activity. Because the HR function plays or should play an important part in running the business, it can make a vital contribution to HCM by developing metrics, analysing and reporting on the implications of the data and proposing and planning HR actions on the basis of that analysis. HCM can also provide information to line managers that will help to improve their effectiveness in managing people and HCM can be used by HR to improve the HR function's own effectiveness. Walters (2006) suggests that 'effective HR processes need to be underpinned by a more rigorous foundation of both quantitative and qualitative analysis than has often traditionally been the case'.

This chapter explores the following aspects of the HR function's involvement with HCM:

▌ the concept of HR specialists as business partners and the relevance of HCM to that concept;

▌ the role of HR in developing metrics and analysing and using the information obtained;

▌ how, with the help of HCM, HR can be strategic and make the business case in order to convince management of the need to take action;

▌ the role of HR in enhancing engagement and commitment;

▌ the need to work with other functions, especially the finance function.

The skills that HR will need to develop and contribute to effective HCM are discussed in Chapter 9.

THE BUSINESS PARTNER CONCEPT AND HCM

The concept of HR practitioners as business partners has seized the imagination of HR people ever since it was first mooted by Ulrich in 1998. In essence, the concept is that, as business partners, HR specialists share responsibility with their line management colleagues for the success of the enterprise and get involved with them in running the business. They must have the capacity to identify business opportunities, to see the broad picture and to understand how their HR role can help to achieve the company's business objectives.

Ulrich suggested that as champions of competitiveness in creating and delivering value, HR professionals carry out the roles of strategic partners, administrative experts, employee champions and change agents. He stated that HR can deliver excellence by becoming a partner with senior and line managers in strategy execution, helping to improve planning from the conference room to the marketplace and that 'HR executives should impel and guide serious discussion of how the company should be organized to carry out its strategy'. He suggested that HR should join forces with operating managers in systematically assessing the importance of any new initiatives they propose and obtaining answers to the following questions: 'Which ones are really aligned with strategy implementation? Which ones should receive immediate attention and which can wait? Which ones, in short, are truly linked to business results?' Ulrich believes that: 'The activities of HR appear to be and often are disconnected from the real work of the organization' and that HR 'should not be defined by what it does but by what it delivers'. The response to this formulation concentrated on the business partner role.

Ulrich and Brockbank (2005a) reformulated Ulrich's 1998 model, listing the following roles:

▌ *Employee advocate* – focuses on the needs of today's employees through listening, understanding and empathizing.

▌ *Human capital developer* – in the role of managing and developing human capital (individuals and teams), focuses on preparing employees to be successful in the future.

▌ *Functional expert* – concerned with the HR practices central to HR value, acts with insight on the basis of the body of knowledge he or she possesses. Some practices are delivered through administrative efficiency (such as technology or process design), and others through policies, menus and interventions. It is necessary to distinguish between the foundation HR practices – recruitment, learning and development, rewards, etc – and the emerging HR practices such as communications, work process and organization design, and executive leadership development.

▌ *Strategic partner* – consists of multiple dimensions: business expert, change agent, strategic HR planner, knowledge manager and consultant, combining these to align HR systems to help accomplish the organization's vision and mission, helping managers to get things done and disseminating learning across the organization.

▌ *Leader* – leads the HR function, collaborating with other functions and providing leadership to them, setting and enhancing the standards for strategic thinking and ensuring corporate governance.

As explained by Ulrich and Brockbank (2005b) the revised formulation is in response to the changes in HR roles they have observed recently. They commented on the importance of the employee advocate role noting that HR professionals spend on average about 19 per cent of their time on employee relations issues and that caring for, listening to and responding to employees remains a centrepiece of HR work. They stated that as a profession HR possesses a body of knowledge that allows HR people to act with insight. Functional expertise enables them to create menus of choice for their business and thus identify options that are consistent with business needs rather than merely ones that they are able to provide. The additional role of human capital developer was introduced because of the increased emphasis on viewing people as critical assets and to recognize the significance of HR's role in developing the workforce. The concept of strategic partner remains broadly the same as before but the additional role of HR leader has been introduced to highlight the importance of leadership by HR specialists of their own function – 'before they can develop other leaders, HR professionals must exhibit the leadership skills they expect in others'.

The Ulrich and Brockbank model focuses on the multi-faceted role of HR people. It serves to correct the impression that Ulrich was simply focusing on them as business partners. This has had the unfortunate effect of implying that that was their only worthwhile function. However, Ulrich cannot be blamed for this. In 1998 he gave equal emphasis to the need for administrative efficiency. And more recently, Syrett (2006) commented that: 'Whatever strategic aspirations senior HR practitioners have, they will amount to nothing if the function they represent cannot deliver the essential transactional services their internal line clients require.'

It has been argued that too much has been made of the business partner model. Tim Miller, Group HR Director of Standard Chartered Bank, as reported by Smethurst (2005), dislikes the term: 'Give me a break!' he says. ' It's so demeaning. How many people in marketing or finance have to say they are a partner in the business? Why do we have to think that we're not an intimate part of the business, just like sales, manufacturing and engineering?' I detest and loathe the term and I won't use it.' Another Group HR Director, Alex Wilson of BT as reported by Pickard (2005), is equally hostile. He says: 'The term worries me to death. HR has to be an integral and fundamental part of developing the strategy of the business. I don't even like the term close to the business because, like business partner it implies we are working alongside our line management colleagues but on a separate track, rather than people management being an integral part of the business.'

Perhaps the vogue for the concept of business partner flows from the inferiority complex that often affects HR practitioners. They want to be recognized as part of the business and calling them business partners seems to meet this need.

Putting the concept into practice has also raised difficulties. The solution adopted by a number of organizations is to attach HR people to operational divisions or departments in the role of business partners, ie working alongside line managers to deliver the expected outcomes. But organizations such as Rowntree & Co (now Nestlé) were doing this 50 years ago and British Bakeries were doing it 40 years ago. And there are many other examples. The personnel specialists 'embedded' in the departments or regions were not called business partners but that was their role.

HCM offers a better way for HR specialists to become embedded in the business. It emphasizes the need to evaluate critically the implications of what has been happening and what can be made to happen. It provides the basis for the formulation and justification of value-adding strategies. It involves those who produce, analyse and disseminate the data (HR specialists) and those responsible for bringing the policies and practices developed through HCM to life (line managers). It helps to ensure, in the words of Alex Wilson, that HR is an integral part of the business.

HR'S ROLE IN DEVELOPING, ANALYSING AND USING HUMAN CAPITAL DATA

HR practitioners are concerned with the development, analysis and use of the following categories of metrics employed in HCM:

- measurements relating to the workforce – composition, attrition, length of service, absence, training activity and effectiveness, level of engagement, opinion-based data, etc;

- measurements of the level and trends in performance achieved by the business and individuals in such terms as financial performance, productivity and customer satisfaction;

- measurements of the impact of HR policies and practices on business performance; what Mercer HR Consulting (Nalbantian *et al*, 2004), call 'business impact modelling';

- measurements of the effectiveness of line managers in applying HR policies;

- measurements of the effectiveness of HR function.

The first step towards HCM is for HR practitioners to develop effectiveness measures of their own contribution to the business and the impact of the people management activities they are responsible for designing and maintaining.

Workforce measurements

Workforce metrics provide the basic data which enables the business to measure certain key characteristics of the people it employs. Some of the key types of workforce measurement have been discussed in the data and measurement chapters above. However, in the context of the relationship between HR and HCM, an understanding of the relationships between people management and workforce metrics is essential. Workforce metrics can focus on those that influence business performance and show the direction in which HR strategy and policies need to be developed to improve the added value obtained from the organization's human capital. It is the job of the HR function to identify the measures that can best be used and ensure that accurate data showing both the current situation and trends can be collected and presented in an easily assimilated form.

What the HR function needs to avoid is simply collecting information because it is there. The purpose of that information should be determined in advance. It should, for example, be understood that information on attrition can generate action to increase the level of retention. Walters (2006) provides an instance of useful analysis at a fairly basic level. In one contact centre environment where staff turnover was running at over 45 per cent, it was noted that newly recruited and trained operators handled, on average, 16 calls per hour. By contrast, those with 12–18 months' service handled, on average, 20 calls per hour. In other words, if staff were retained for 12–18 months their productivity increased by 25 per cent. On this basis, it is possible to begin to develop a business case for significant measures designed to improve staff retention.

Measurements of performance

HCM is more than simply measuring various workforce characteristics and trends, although this is important. HCM is only truly effective if the measurement extends to the impact of HR policies on business and individual performance so that outcomes can be evaluated and guidance obtained on future strategy. The HR function must therefore understand the drivers of performance in the organization and the measurements that can be made available to assess performance levels and trends. Examples of drivers include:

▮ time to market (the pipeline) in a pharmaceutical firm;

▮ development of new markets in a marketing firm;

▮ delivering quality to customers in a manufacturing firm;

▮ client acquisition and retention in a consultancy;

▮ product development in an insurance company;

▮ innovation in a software firm;

▮ shareholder (or City) opinion in a public company;

▮ customer satisfaction levels in a retail organization;

▮ response rates in a mail order firm;

▮ maintaining close control of costs in any firm.

HR can find out what the drivers are by being there when business issues are discussed (and contributing to the discussion) and by finding out the answers to questions such as: What do you believe drives the success of this organization?, What has it got to be good at doing?, What are the key elements in the four quadrants of the balanced scorecard covering customer perspective, internal perspective, innovation and learning perspective and financial perspective? It is important to get involved in the business as this is the only way in which proper understanding of the drivers can be achieved. If this involvement can be extended to taking part in the development of all parts of the balanced scorecard (not just the learning or people perspective) so much the better.

Having established the drivers the next question to be asked is: How do you measure success? The aim is to establish the key performance indicators. These can be grouped under the following headings:

▮ financial measures, eg shareholder value, added value, economic value added (EVA), sales turnover, income generated;

▮ productivity measures, eg added value per unit or employee, sales turnover per unit or employee, units of output per employee;

▌ operational impact or effectiveness measures, eg successful management or completion of projects, customers or clients acquired and retained, new products launched, new markets opened, value of new business;

▌ customer service, eg levels of satisfaction, service levels, complaints.

Decisions have also to be made about how individual or team performance is to be measured. This means examining the performance management processes in place and establishing the extent to which they provide reliable data on levels of performance, and importantly, trends in those levels.

Measurements of the impact of HR policies and practices on performance

These are the critical measures which provide guidance on the effectiveness of past actions and on the direction of future actions. They are the most rewarding but also the hardest to obtain. It is relatively easy to measure performance, it is more difficult to establish correlations between HR activities and results and even more difficult to determine causation – what actions or factors specifically created the change in performance.

An example of a model developed by HR with technical help is provided by the Nationwide Building Society, which devised its Genome II human capital investment model to quantify the impact that employee retention has on customer satisfaction and business performance (see Figure 6.3 in Chapter 6). This model uses data from existing sources such as employee opinion surveys, customer satisfaction indices, business performance statistics and employee metrics covering turnover, length of service and absence. Use of the model enabled the Nationwide Building Society to prove statistically that the more committed the employee the happier the customer. It is possible to use data modelling to predict the impact that a change in one factor affecting employee commitment would have on customer satisfaction and ultimately on business performance. For example, increasing employee satisfaction with basic pay by 5 per cent would produce an overall rise in customer satisfaction of 0.5 per cent and an increase in personal loan sales of 2.3 per cent. The Genome project has helped to focus activity on:

▌ recruitment and retention;

▌ a greater understanding of employee commitment – that is, what is the difference between those employees who want to be in the organization, need to be there or feel they ought to be there;

▌ transparency and flexibility of reward;

▌ first-line management development and coaching/mentoring to deliver the emotional as well as the task management aspects of the role;

▌ promotion of recognition and *ad hoc* or spontaneous rewards for employees – visible and tangible celebrations of success;

▌ development of an organizational culture where managers and employees are emotionally committed to and demonstrate the right behaviours.

Measurements of the effectiveness of line managers

HCM metrics can provide information on how effectively line managers are carrying out their people management responsibilities that indicates areas for improvement and where guidance, help or further training is required. At the Nationwide Building Society regular reports are made to area managers on key drivers. These are presented graphically on dashboards as illustrated in Figure 6.4 in Chapter 6.

Measurements of the effectiveness of HR

As Mayo (2006) comments, measurements of the effectiveness of HR are not to do with human capital in general. But they are still relevant to evaluating how effective HR process is in contributing to HCM. Mayo refers to service levels and cost ratios in providing HR services and argues for measures of value added from the function.

It is necessary to evaluate the contribution of the HR function to ensure that it is effective at both the strategic level and in terms of service delivery and support. In evaluation it is useful to remember the distinction made by Tsui and Gomez-Mejia (1988) between *process criteria* – how well things are done, and *output criteria* – the effectiveness of the end-result. A 'utility analysis' approach as described by Boudreau (1988) can be used. This focuses on the impact of HR activities measured wherever possible in financial terms (*quantity*), improvements in the *quality* of those activities, and *cost/benefit* (the minimization of the cost of the activities in relation to the benefits they provide).

Huselid *et al* (1997) believe that HR effectiveness has two dimensions: (1) *strategic HRM* – the delivery of services in a way which supports the implementation of the firm's strategy; (2) *technical HRM* – the delivery of HR basics such as recruitment, compensation and benefits.

The following points about measuring HR performance have been made by Likierman (2005):

▌ Agree objectives against budget assumptions, this will ensure that HR's role reflects changes in strategy implementation.

▌ Use more sophisticated measures – get underneath the data and look not only at the figures but at the reasons behind them.

▌ Use comparisons imaginatively, including internal and external benchmarking;

▌ Improve feedback through face-to-face discussion rather than relying on questionnaires;

▌ Be realistic about what performance measures can deliver – many measurement problems can be mitigated, not solved.

The HR scorecard developed by Beatty *et al* (2003) gives a useful framework for measuring HR performance. It follows the same principle as a corporate balanced scorecard, ie it emphasizes the need for a balanced presentation and analysis of data. The four headings of the HR scorecard are:

▌ *HR competencies* – administrative expertise, employee advocacy, strategy execution and change agency;

▌ *HR practices* – communication, work design, selection, development, measurement and rewards;

▌ *HR systems* – alignment, integration and differentiation;

▌ *HR deliverables* – workforce mindset, technical knowledge, and workforce behaviour.

These are all influenced by the factors that determine the strategic success of the organization, ie operational excellence, product leadership and customer intimacy.

THE ROLE OF HR IN ENHANCING JOB ENGAGEMENT AND COMMITMENT

'Engagement' has become a key concept recently. Anyone concerned in people management needs to be aware of what the terms 'engagement' and 'commitment' mean – they are often used loosely – and what needs to be done about them to enhance the value added by human capital.

Job engagement and organizational commitment defined

Job engagement takes place when people are committed to their work and motivated to achieve high levels of performance. The Hay Group (Murlis, 2005) defines engaged performance as: 'A result that is achieved by stimulating employees' enthusiasm for their work and directing it towards organizational success. This result can only be achieved when employers offer an implied contract to their employees that elicits specific positive behaviours aligned with the organization's goals.'

Organizational commitment is about identification with the goals and values of the organization, a desire to belong to the organization and a willingness to display effort on its behalf.

Creating a great place to work

Enhancing job engagement and commitment ensures that the organization is perceived as being 'a great place to work', ie it becomes an 'employer of choice'. On the basis of their longitudinal research in 12 companies Purcell *et al* (2003) concluded that:

> What seems to be happening is that successful firms are able to meet people's needs both for a good job and to work 'in a great place'. They create good work and a conducive working environment. In this way they become an 'employer of choice'. People will want to work there because their individual needs are met – for a good job with prospects linked to training, appraisal and working with a good boss who listens and gives some autonomy but helps with coaching and guidance.

The criteria used by *The Sunday Times* in identifying 'The 100 best companies to work for, 2005' were:

▌ leadership at senior management level;

▌ 'my manager' – local management on a day-to-day basis;

▌ personal growth – opportunities to learn, grow and be challenged;

▌ well-being – balanced work–life issues;

▌ 'my team' – immediate colleagues; giving something back – to society and the local community;

▌ 'my company' – the way it treats staff;

▌ 'fair deal' – pay and benefits.

To create a great place to work the HR department initiates policies and programmes that take account of these criteria and provides guidance and advice helping to develop the image of the organization so that it is recognized as one that achieves results, delivers quality products and services, behaves ethically and provides good conditions of employment.

Positive discretionary behaviour

HR is particularly concerned with furthering job engagement and there is a close link between high levels of engagement and positive discretionary behaviour, As described by Purcell *et al* (2003) discretionary behaviour refers to the choices that people at work often have on the way they do the job and the amount of effort, care, innovation and productive behaviour they display. It can be positive when people 'go the extra mile' to achieve high levels of performance. It can be negative when they exercise their discretion to slack at their work. Discretionary behaviour is hard for the employer to define and then monitor and control the amount required. But positive discretionary behaviour is more likely to happen when people are engaged with their work.

The propositions made by Purcell *et al* on discretionary behaviour were that:

▌ Performance-related practices only work if they positively induce discretionary behaviour, once basic staffing requirements have been met.

∥ Discretionary behaviour is more likely to occur when enough individuals have commitment to their organization and/or when they feel motivated to do so and/or when they gain high levels of job satisfaction.

∥ Commitment, motivation and job satisfaction, either together or separately, will be higher when people positively experience the application of HR policies concerned with creating an able workforce, motivating valued behaviours and providing opportunities to participate.

∥ This positive experience will be higher if the wide range of HR policies necessary to develop ability, motivation, and opportunity are both in place and are mutually reinforcing.

∥ The way HR and reward policies and practices are implemented by frontline managers and the way top-level espoused values and organizational cultures are enacted by them will enhance or weaken the effect of HR policies in triggering discretionary behaviour by influencing attitudes.

∥ The experience of success seen in performance outcomes helps reinforce positive attitudes.

Total reward policies

HR can further job engagement and productive discretionary behaviour by getting the organization to adopt total reward policies. This means combining transactional rewards – tangible rewards arising from transactions between the employer and employees concerning pay and benefits – and relational rewards – intangible rewards concerned with learning and development and the work experience. This combination can have a much more powerful effect than if the focus were on one or the other. A total reward approach is holistic, reliance is not placed on a few reward mechanisms operating in isolation, and account is taken of every way in which people can be rewarded and obtain satisfaction through their work. The aim is to maximize the combined impact of a wide range of reward initiatives on motivation, job engagement and organizational commitment.

A model of total reward developed by Towers Perrin is shown in Figure 8.1.

The upper two quadrants – pay and benefits – represent the transactional rewards that are financial in nature and are essential to recruit

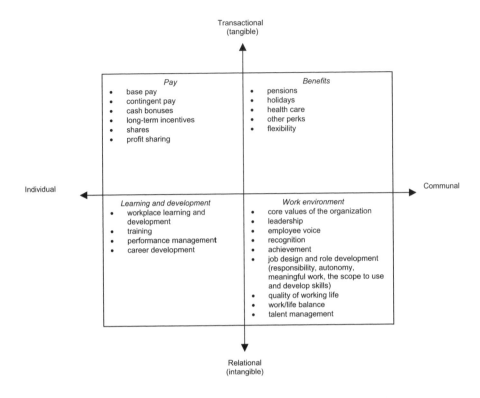

Source: Armstrong, M and Brown, D (2006)

Figure 8.1 The Towers Perrin model of total reward

and retain staff but which can be easily copied by competitors. By contrast, the relational (non-financial) rewards produced by the lower two quadrants are more difficult to imitate and increase the value of the upper two quadrants. The real power, as Thompson (2002) states, comes when organizations combine relational and transactional rewards.

Using measurements

HR can help to enhance engagement and commitment by running surveys such as the example in the Appendix (see page 192). These can reveal issues that can be addressed by a total reward strategy. This will only be effective if the performance of the organization is measured in each of the four quadrants of the Towers Perrin total reward model shown in Figure 8.1. Quantitative metrics such as those listed in the Appendix (see pages 181–84) can be used for this purpose, but qualitative assessments can also be valuable. It should never be assumed that HCM only works in quantified terms.

THE STRATEGIST ROLE

As strategists, HR professionals address major long-term organizational issues concerning the management and development of people and the employment relationship. They are guided by the business plans of the organization but they also contribute to the formulation of the business plans. This is achieved by ensuring that top managers focus on the HR implications of those plans and are persuaded to develop business strategies that make the best use of the organization's human capital. They emphasize, in the words of Hendry and Pettigrew (1986), that people are a strategic resource for the achievement of competitive advantage. But they will be in a much stronger position to do this if they can back up their proposals with human capital data that demonstrates that added value will be created. They have to prepare a business case using this data and proceed to exercise their powers of persuasion which, however, will be more convincing if the supporting data is there.

MAKING THE BUSINESS CASE

A business case sets out the reasons why a proposed course of action will benefit the business, how it will provide that benefit and how much it will cost. The case is made either in added-value terms (ie the income generated by the proposal will significantly exceed the cost of implementing it), or on the basis of the return on investment (ie the cost of the investment, say in training, is justified by the financial returns in such areas as increased productivity).

A business case will be enhanced if:

▮ Data as part of a human capital approach is available on the impact the proposal is likely to make on key areas of the organization's operations, eg customer service levels, quality, shareholder value, productivity, income generation, innovation, skills development, talent management.

▌ It can be shown that the proposal will increase the business' competitive edge, for example enlarging the skill base or multiskilling to ensure that it can achieve competitive advantage through innovation and/or reducing time to market.

▌ There is proof that the innovation has already worked well within the organization (perhaps as a pilot scheme) or represents 'good practice' that is likely to be transferable to the organization.

▌ It can be implemented without too much trouble, for example not taking up a lot of managers' time, or not meeting with strong opposition from line managers, employees or trade unions (it is as well to check the likely reaction before launching a proposal).

▌ It will add to the reputation of the company by showing that it is a 'world class' organization, ie what it does is as good as, if not better than, the world leaders in the sector in which the business operates (a promise that publicity will be achieved through articles in professional journals, press releases and conference presentations will help).

▌ It will enhance the 'employer brand' of the company by making it a 'best place to work'.

▌ The proposal is brief, to the point and well argued – it should take no more than five minutes to present orally and should be summarized in writing on the proverbial one side of one sheet of A4 paper (supplementary details can be included in appendices).

Making the business case is obviously easier where management is preconditioned to agree to the proposition. For example, it is not hard to convince top managers that performance-related pay is a good thing – they may well be receiving bonus payments themselves and believe, rightly or wrongly, that because it motivates them it will motivate everyone else. Talent management is another process where top management needs little persuasion that things need to be done to enhance and preserve the talent flow, although they will have to be convinced that in practice, innovations will achieve that aim. Performance management may be slightly more difficult because it is hard to demonstrate that it can produce measurable improvements in performance, but senior managers are predisposed towards an approach which at least promises to improve the level of performance.

The toughest area for justification in added-value returns can be expenditure on learning and development programmes. This is where an ROI approach as discussed in Chapter 7 is desirable. The business case for learning and development should demonstrate how learning, training and development programmes will meet business needs. Kearns and Miller (1997) go so far as to claim that: 'If a business objective cannot be cited as a basis for designing training and development, then no training and development should be offered.'

The areas of the business strategy that depend on talented people should be analysed. The organization's strategic plans and their impact on knowledge and skill requirements should also be noted. For example, these might include the development of a high-performance culture, productivity improvements, the innovation and launch of new products or services, achieving better levels of service delivery to customers, or the extended use of IT or other forms of technology. Any proposed learning and training interventions should specify how they will contribute to the achievement of these strategic goals.

A cost/benefit analysis is required comparing the benefits expressed in quantified terms as far as possible that will result from the learning activity. The case for investing in learning and development can refer to any of the following potential benefits:

▌ improving individual, team and corporate performance in terms of output, quality, speed and overall productivity;

▌ attracting high-quality employees by offering them learning and development opportunities, increasing their levels of competence and enhancing their skills, thus enabling them to obtain more job satisfaction, to gain higher rewards and to progress within the organization;

▌ providing additional non-financial rewards (growth and career opportunities) as part of a total reward policy;

▌ improving operational flexibility by extending the range of skills possessed by employees (multiskilling);

▌ increasing the commitment of employees by encouraging them to identify with the mission and objectives of the organization;

∎ helping to manage change by increasing understanding of the reasons for change and providing people with the knowledge and skills they need to adjust to new situations;

∎ providing line managers with the skills required to manage and develop their people;

∎ helping to develop a positive culture in the organization, one, for example, oriented towards performance improvement;

∎ providing higher levels of service to customers;

∎ minimizing learning costs (reducing the length of learning curves).

Gaining support and commitment

HR practitioners mainly get results by persuasion based on credibility and expertise. As Guest and Hoque (1994) note: 'By exerting influence, HR managers help to shape the framework of HR policy and practice.' Although line managers make the day-to-day decisions, it is still vital for HR specialists to have influencing skills. But there is a constant danger of HR professionals being so overcome by the beauty and truth of their bright idea that they expect everyone else – management and employees alike – to fall for it immediately. This is not how it is. Management and employees can create blockages and barriers and their support and commitment need to be gained, which is not always easy.

The support of top management is achievable by processes of marketing the HR function and persuasion. Boards and senior managers, like anyone else, are more likely to be persuaded to take a course of action if it can be demonstrated that it will meet both the needs of the organization and their own personal needs. In addition, the proposal must be backed by a realistic and persuasive business case that spells out the benefits and the costs and, as far as possible, is justified either in added-value terms, or on the basis of a return on investment.

WORKING WITH THE OTHER FUNCTIONS

As Duncan Brown, Assistant Director of the CIPD (2006) has pointed out: 'The responsibility and use of human capital information cannot, as one participant in our research put it, "remain in an HR ghetto". We have to engage managers and other functions in improving and using this information.' It is necessary to get involved with line managers in interpreting the data and with other functions in preparing human capital information. Measuring the impact of human capital on business performance requires comparisons between human capital inputs and financial outcomes. This means that HR has to work closely with finance to obtain agreement on what financial measures are appropriate and available and to collaborate on the production and analysis of data. This is a true business partnership.

9

The skills HR specialists need for HCM

There is already a debate emerging about the readiness of HR practitioners to develop the skills necessary to support the delivery of effective HCM. Mayo (2004) has commented that the professional HR practitioner needs some essential tools to be able to:

- understand and articulate the meaning of 'value' and 'added value' from the perspective of a support function;

- quantify both costs and returns in relation to people and organization management;

- be confident and competent in justifying investments that relate to people.

Clearly, as demonstrated in earlier chapters, human capital evaluation and measurement requires a set of skills around metrics and statistics that have not traditionally been included in HR professional development. Many of the practitioners interviewed for this book did not think this was an issue as they were readily able to find statistical expertise from other departments or available to buy in as consultancy services.

However, whereas undoubtedly the more specialized statistical skills of data analysis and the administrative skills of data entry and collection can be bought in, one of the most important challenges is about linking all the organizational metrics together and identifying both correlations and, ideally, causal relationships, to demonstrate that the way things are done has an impact on performance. This means that, although they may not need to have specialized skills, HR people will need to understand the meaning behind the metrics to rise to this challenge.

For example, it will usually be more cost effective to buy in the skills to administer, collect data and analyse the results of an employee attitude survey. However, understanding what the results of that survey mean for the business and the impact of improving the results will have on business performance is a skill that cannot readily be bought in from outside the company and should ideally be present within the HR department. Similarly, communicating the results to the workforce and agreeing actions for improvements will need the input of specialist HR knowledge.

Members of the CIPD's Human Capital Panel debating this issue concluded that this is not just about developing skills within HR, it is also about developing real HCM capability across the organization. This means that although a skills base to understand and communicate on metrics is required in the HR team, it is not necessarily HR specialists who need to provide it. What is perhaps more worthwhile is reviewing HR skills to identify the gaps in the required knowledge and expertise and then reviewing what skills are available across the organization in other functions that can be used to fill these gaps. They argued that because HCM is an organization-wide phenomenon and should not be solely an HR issue, it is both easier and appropriate to develop the skill set needed from a cross-functional team with representatives from the line as well as other specialist areas such as internal communications.

There are many benefits in developing a cross-functional human capital team, not least of which is that members of the team will act as ambassadors in their own departments to get the human capital message disseminated around the organization. In addition, it may prove more cost effective than using external consultants.

Using external consultants to plug gaps in the HR skill set may be a short-term solution but will not necessarily help in creating the right set of skills for long-term HCM. Although consultants may be a rich source of technical expertise or be able to offer good advice on the development of systems, they will not necessarily have sufficient understanding of the business to make the connections between the metrics or to identify the key business drivers. However, in many cases some external advice is necessary both to kick start the process and to enable organizations to make progress and indeed develop HCM skills internally.

Ultimately, creating the right skill set will depend on the circumstances of the organization and the resources available to it.

CLOSING THE SKILLS GAP

The consensus among both practitioners and commentators is that there is, at present, a skills gap in HR that needs closing if HR is going to fulfil its role in developing effective HCM. However, this gap is not necessarily going to be closed by employing more HR people. Instead, capability can be developed within existing HR departments by developing the skills of HR people themselves and supplementing these with more specialist technical skills from other functions where possible, coupled with advice and guidance from external consultants at critical stages along the human capital pathway. The important thing for HR people is to build the understanding of how to go about engaging with and informing the business of the contribution of people and what actions will maximize this contribution and drive business performance. It is apparent from the above that to do this they will have to become adept at creating enduring multi-functional teams to consider human capital issues.

Syrett (2006) comments:

> The main challenge – if the organization is going to get a return on its human capital – is in building up a cadre of business-facing HR staff with the partnering skills to apply the new insights to the needs of the business. This is the payoff without which all human capital activity is a useless waste of time...
>
> Human capital assessment places a premium on the partnership skills of business-facing HR staff...
>
> The tools and methodologies that underpin any human capital measurement system lie at the heart of its effectiveness... HR practitioners will need to work closely with business units to identify how the richer data yielded by enhanced human capital measurement will help line managers anticipate developing trends that might undermine the commitment, engagement or retention of their staff.

What appears to be needed in HR departments therefore is a mixture of the business-focused and strategic skills that have long been argued for by the proponents of strategic HRM. These include the more technical skills of understanding and presenting complex data coupled with the ability to use this data to build credible arguments to demonstrate the impact and contribution of people and people management activities. This does not necessarily imply a radical change in the development of HR but rather something more evolutionary designed to build capability. However, from the knowledge and evidence we have been able to generate we can offer below a template that might guide this process within organizations.

DEVELOPING A NEW TEMPLATE FOR HR

A number of questions are often posed in discussion on the skills HR need to deliver HCM. These questions are concerned not only with the nature and types of skills that HR people need but also how they will acquire and develop them within the career paths open to them. The questions being debated in the HR profession include the following:

▌ Where are the HR people of the future going to come from?

▌ If people are not developing the necessary skills in a traditional HR career path how will we develop them?

▌ Do we need to develop a highly training human capital specialist or do we need to give the HR department a broader understanding of human capital issues?

▌ What kind of relationships do we need to establish with other functions to develop the capacity of HCM within the HR function?

▌ What skills do line managers need to acquire for effective HCM?

▌ What will the relationships between HR and the line look like in the future?

In the course of discussions with human capital specialists in a variety of organizations it has become clear that a minority have followed a traditional career path, rising through the ranks of HR to specialize in human capital. For example, Grieg Aiken, whose post of Head of Employee Research and Measurement at the Royal Bank of Scotland was created specifically for the task, has a background in corporate and business lending rather than HR. Roger Cooper, who at the time of writing was leading the human capital initiative for Centrica, has an engineering background. Other specialists have emerged from marketing or other functions. The answer to the HR versus human capital specialist question seems to be that it depends what will fit the purpose of the business. Often a specialist post is needed, largely because human capital needs some kind of HR champion prepared to get started on the difficult tasks of identifying the data and analysing and communicating it as described above. This has definitely been the case in most of the organizations interviewed where a definite human capital champion has emerged to drive the initiative. This post needs to be fit for purpose and will often change over time as HCM becomes more established and more sophisticated. This specialist may or may not be an HR specialist but will have to engage with the HR department to generate the information and understanding he or she will need to fulfil the role. In addition, it will also be important for HR staff to develop sufficient understanding to influence and direct the output from these specialist posts.

The most recent stage of the CIPD research investigating the link between HR and business performance carried out at Bath University (Kinnie *et al*, 2006), demonstrates a number of demands on the HR practitioners for effective HCM. This research demonstrates that HR processes need to be embedded within the core business processes. HR practitioners therefore need in-depth knowledge of how projects are managed within the business and a clear operational awareness of how the business functions. Only if this understanding is present will they be able to design HR practices that will support the knowledge creation process and the conversion of that knowledge into organizational value.

The knowledge and skills required within the HR function to implement and operate a full HCM programme are diverse and will differ between organizations and situations. However, the following list is a general framework of the requirements and demands that HR practitioners are increasingly required to deliver on.

Understanding of the business – its strategies and key drivers

This is an essential requirement. As discussed in the previous chapter, the business partner model has perhaps been overemphasized.

Tim Miller, Director of People, Property and Assurance at Standard Chartered Bank, debating the issue with the CIPD Human Capital Panel stressed he did not want business partners he wanted players. He went on to say:

> The starting point for building top class HR players is to identify the talent needed to be successful. And here I define talent as recurring patterns of thought, feelings and behaviours which are linked to success in an HR role. Without this, it is much harder to develop and grow them. Identifying talent in this way expands the range of backgrounds from which top class HR professionals can be drawn. Being an HR player requires new capabilities including strong analytical skills, empathy and sensitivity to understand business issues and powerful problem solving abilities. It's also probably the case that these new capabilities go hand in hand with greater intellectual weight and academic disciplines. Once HR talent has been identified we need to invest in those HR people through development and planned exposure to the business – proper career management and development in other words!

An appreciation of how HR strategy interacts with the business strategy

In their 2002 report on the research commissioned by the CIPD, Scarborough and Elias argued that one of the most important aspects of human capital is that it acts as a bridging concept between HR strategy and business strategy, defining the link between HR practice and business performance in terms of assets rather than process. HR therefore needs the skills to engage effectively in the strategic decision-making process to ensure that these decisions are made on the basis of all the information available to the organization. Failure to do so will once again mean that one of the most important assets that should be helping to define business strategy – human capital – is under-represented.

Knowledge of the data

Collection of data is an administrative task that need not be done by HR practitioners. Similarly, data analysis is a specialized task that may require buying in or specialized skills. However, HR practitioners do need sufficient knowledge of the nature of data, data collection techniques and data analysis to identify what data already exists and how this might be used. In particular they need to be able to identify data that will enable them to measure organizational and individual performance and the performance of HR. A wealth of information is available to HR in the form of performance data, salary details, training data, absence, retention, accident rates, etc, all of which can be generated at the touch of a button thanks to the extensive use of computerized HR information systems. However, just because the data exists does not mean it tells us anything useful and HR people need to be able to make value judgements about the relative worth of the information available to them.

Understanding of what information managers need

In order to be able to develop the sort of positive relationships with line managers described above, HR practitioners need to provide managers with information that has meaning for them and how they perform in their jobs. Just giving managers information is not enough, this has to be accompanied by adequate explanation of what it means and the actions that may have to be taken as a result. Because line managers are now delivering so much HR activity the skills they need have changed. Human capital information provides HR practitioners with the tools to convince line managers of the value of implementing HR practice, and implementing it well, by demonstrating the impact and the value for them in terms of their own performance,

Knowledge of how to collect and analyse data

The actual collection and analysis can be carried out by others, but HR people need sufficient understanding to appreciate how this is done. One of the common problems identified in discussions with practitioners was the problem of comparing data collected from different systems or using different methodologies. Many concluded that this was a direct result of HR's inability to adequately specify their requirements from HR information systems in the past. There is also the added danger that without adequate knowledge of the nature of data collection and analysis, line managers' expectations for information will not be fulfilled, which will in turn damage their trust in the information they are given.

Skills in presenting data and reporting on the outcomes of analysis

This is perhaps one of the most crucial skills for HR people. Being able to present their data in a way that will convince line managers and business leaders will need both presentation skills and influencing skills. Discussion among the members of CIPD Human Capital Panel concluded that information alone was insufficient. HR needs to be competent at building a credible argument if they are going to demonstrate the real contribution of human capital. Because much of the data and many of the measures are 'soft' and open to interpretation it is important that it can be presented in the language of business and in a way that will have relevance for the intended audience. This may also mean presenting the same information in several different ways for different audiences. Some expertise in presenting information graphically and at least a working knowledge of advanced statistical techniques such as correlation, regression analysis, factor analysis and multi-variant analysis would be an advantage.

Skills in working as part of a management team

Human capital is not the sole preserve of the HR function and effective HCM will require action to be taken as a team. HR people therefore must develop the skills to work as part of this team, using strategic decision-making and influencing skills to put their case across and business skills and knowledge of the business processes to demonstrate how this impacts on the business.

Skills in working with the finance function

Relationships between HR and finance have often been uneasy. However, much of the impetus for better human capital information has come from the financial community, who are increasingly expressing a need for better understanding of intangible value. While we do not want to impose rigid accountancy models on human capital, HR practitioners do need at least to understand the language of finance and be able to express human capital information in a way that will have relevance. This means being able to justify investment in people management practice and the development of human capital in terms of return by identifying and articulating how this will be evaluated and how it relates to identifiable business drivers.

HR VERSUS LINE MANAGER SKILLS

It is not just HR skills that need attention to develop HCM in an organization. The skills of line managers also need to be scrutinized.

Research for the CIPD by Bath University (Hutchinson and Purcell, 2003) makes the case that it is not people management policy in itself that contributes to business performance but rather the way these polices are implemented and brought to life by line managers. As a result they identified a set of skills for line managers that need to be present for good business performance. These include the so-called soft skills of listening, coaching, mentoring, involvement and communication.

HCM too has implications for the skills of line managers. HCM takes as its central premise that people are a resource to be invested in and this has significant implications for the traditional HR cycle of recruitment, development, career management and exit. A resource that has been invested in and nurtured is not as easily dispensable as one with which a solely transactional relationships exists. Recruitment means looking for potential rather than a set of existing skills or competencies. This makes it even more important that line managers are involved in people management decisions and more importantly acquire the skills to enable them to carry out this aspect of the job effectively. The CIPD research found that all too often managers were not only denied the opportunity to acquire the skills but also were not given enough time within their role to carry out the people management side.

The changing nature of the relationships between HR and the line has promoted an evolutionary change in HR skills over the last few years. Approximately 80 per cent of HR activity carried out by HR managers in the past is now delivered by line managers. This has changed not only the skills needed by both sides but also the nature of the role, with HR often responsible for the design of process but not the delivery.

In addition, the rise of the business partner model means that HR people now rely much more heavily on consultancy skills and persuasion rather than authority to get line managers to deliver this activity effectively. Business therefore increasingly needs HR people who can manage the line rather than become pseudo line managers themselves by taking on more hands-on people management activity. As one member of the CIPD panel commented:

What is needed is some sort of template of how the best HR managers are informed of what business is demanding and expecting of them. This need not be some kind of big scary change but rather identifying the process by which people become engaged with the business. We need to give people strategies about how they can go about developing the sort of relationships within their business which is going to inform this work.

CONCLUSIONS

HR needs to develop a number of new skills for effective HCM. However, this is more likely to be an evolutionary than a revolutionary process. Syrett (2006) emphasizes that:

The main challenge – if the organization is to get a return on its investment in human capital – is in building up a cadre of business-facing HR staff with the partnering skills to apply the new insights to the needs of the business, this is the payoff without which all human capital activity is a useless waste of time. It is also important for HR to form enduring relationships with line managers to ensure the HR function builds the capability it needs for effective human capital management. The business partner model is popular with the HR profession but may not go far enough to achieve this.

10

The future of HCM

Despite all the examples we have been able to give of good HCM, the reality is that HCM is still in its infancy. No more than a handful of organizations in the UK have developed sophisticated HCM techniques. Many others are using measurements, both quantitative and qualitative, to good purpose but have just embarked on the journey that leads to the systematic use of these measurements to guide business decision making on people matters.

THE VIRTUES OF HCM

The virtuous future of HCM have been extolled by many commentators, for example:

▌ HCM is: 'The total development of human potential expressed as organizational value'. HCM is clearly seen and respected as an equal business partner at senior levels and is 'holistic, organization-wide and systems-based' as well as being strategic and concerned with adding value (Kearns, 2005a).

▌ HCM is about 'harnessing people measures to drive business performance' (Penna Consulting, 2003).

▌ 'Human capital management must be appreciated as a distinct measurement and investment-led business approach that recognises and adjusts to traditional functional behaviours but asserts itself, nevertheless, as a central component of business planning and operations' (Donkin, 2005).

▌ HCM data 'informs and inspires the best policies' (Syrett, 2006).

Nicholas Higgins, Chief Executive of Valuentis, explains why he believes it is important (Higgins, 2005):

> If HR wishes to have strategic 'clout' then it has to do measurement and 'do measurement' well. If it doesn't it won't. People are simultaneously assets, resources and potential liabilities. HR is a corporate function with two main objectives: optimising people performance and minimising operational risk. This is no small feat, which is why HR faces such a challenge. And neither of these objectives can be achieved without some measurement. Without it, optimising people performance becomes an impossible concept to realise, with the danger of either over- or under-investment in people management practice and/or people development. Minimising operational risk without investment means HR is perpetually reacting to events rather than proactively avoiding them.

QUESTION MARKS ABOUT HCM

For some people, there is still a large question mark about the concept of HCM. Some people feel the term is dehumanizing. As Scarborough and Elias (2002) discovered in their research, many managers, especially HR managers, feel uncomfortable with a perspective that seems to reduce employees to economic units. Scarborough and Elias also noted that:

> The reasons for managerial backwardness in this field relate in large part to the paradoxical characteristics of human capital. On the one hand, employee skills and competencies make a critical contribution to business performance. On the other hand, the features that make human capital so critical are the very same features that inhibit evaluation. Thus, one of the features of human capital that makes it so crucial to firm performance is the flexibility and creativity of individuals, their ability to develop skills over time and to respond in a motivated way to different contexts. Much of this depends on the acquisition and application of tacit knowledge; that is knowledge that we cannot readily articulate but is acquired through a process of situated learning. It follows from

this that human capital is to a large extent non-standardised, tacit, dynamic, context dependent and embodied in people.

David Longbotham, Group Director of HR, DSG International (Longbotham, 2005), expresses doubts about the notion of statuary people metrics:

> The HR function is better employed in providing leadership on people matters as a means of delivering competitive advantage. That is where value is added. Frankly, the only value added that statutory people metrics will deliver is to consultancies and academics. I believe we should resist demands for a common set of employee metrics in the annual report. HR is increasingly central to every management decision, reflecting the pivotal role of people in the delivery of business objectives. Playing the numbers game won't raise the profile or improve the performance of the HR profession, nor will it secure HR's place as a strategic partner to the chief executive.

Be that as it may, as yet, many HR people seem to be unconvinced or unable to act on the evidence available and senior management may only have heard about it because of the aborted proposal for OFRs (Operational and Financial Reviews). The future of HCM is dependent on the resolution of this and a number of the other issues discussed in this chapter, namely:

▌ the link between HCM and business strategy;

▌ defining the relationship between HCM and business performance;

▌ convincing senior management that it is important;

▌ understanding and fulfilling the needs of the investment community for better information on intangible value;

▌ enlisting the interest and involvement of line management;

▌ convincing HR specialists that it is important and feasible;

▌ staging the development of HCM;

▌ developing HR skills in HCM;

▌ understanding what is meant by obtaining added value from people;

▌ understanding what is meant by regarding people as assets;

▌ selecting the measures;

▮ analysing and evaluating the data;

▮ external reporting that has value for investors and others and recognizes the value of human capital information.

THE LINK BETWEEN HCM AND BUSINESS STRATEGY

The Accounting for People Task Force (2003) defined HCM as: 'An approach to people management that treats it as a high level strategic issue rather than an organizational matter to be left to the HR people'. And one of the key questions often asked about HCM is: 'What are the key people issues driving the business agenda?' It is often asserted that HCM and business strategy are closely linked and that an HCM approach provides guidance on both HR and business strategy. For example:

▮ By linking good HR practice and strategic management to human capital measurement firms are able to make a number of better informed decisions that will help to ensure long-term business success (Scarborough and Elias, 2002).

▮ The aim is to have a 'robust people strategy mapped to the business strategy' (Manocha, 2005).

▮ The prime purpose of HCM is to establish 'an employment proposition that links the work of employees to strategy and profits' (Donkin, 2005).

The issue is to determine what this link is and how to make it work. A bland statement that HCM informs HR strategy which in turn informs business strategy tells us nothing about what is involved in practice. If we are not careful we are saying no more than that all business strategic plans for innovation, growth and price/cost leadership depend on people for their implementation. This is not a particularly profound or revealing statement and is in the same category as the discredited cliché: 'Our people are our greatest asset.' We must try and be more specific, otherwise we are only doing things – more training, succession planning, performance management, performance-related pay and so on – in the hope rather than the expectation that they will improve business results.

One way of being more specific is to use HCM assessments of the impact of HR practices on performance to justify these practices and improve the likelihood that they will work. The future of HCM as a strategic management process largely depends on getting this done.

A second way of specifying the link is to explore in more detail the people implications of business strategy and, conversely, the business implications of HR strategy. This can be done by analysing the elements of the business strategy and the business drivers and deciding on the HR supporting activities and HCM data required, as illustrated in Table 10.1.

A third, and potentially the most productive, way of linking HR and business strategy is to relate business results to HR policies and practices to determine where the best ROI will be obtained, as discussed below.

ESTABLISHING THE LINK BETWEEN HR PRACTICE AND BUSINESS PERFORMANCE

In the future, one of the most important developments in HCM will be the methodologies required to establish causal links between HR policies and practices and measures of business performance, as the following comments underline:

▌ 'HCM demands the measurement of human assets and an evaluation of their overall impact on corporate performance' (IRS, 2004).

▌ 'The key requirement here is not simply to assess the overall value of human capital, but also to develop an understanding of the underpinning elements and dynamics that translate notional human capital into genuine business value' (Walters, 2006).

▌ 'Improving the productive capacity of a workforce is difficult to achieve without a comprehensive understanding of the linkage between employee inputs and profitable results' (Donkin, 2005).

Defining the link between business performance and HR practices affecting the availability, engagement and development of human capital is the ultimate goal of HCM and the most difficult one to achieve. The aim is to be able to say on the basis of measurement: 'When we do

Table 10.1 Analysis of business strategy and business drivers

	Content	HR supporting activities	Supporting data required
Business strategy	Growth of revenue/ profit Maximize shareholder value Growth through acquisitions/mergers Growth in production/servicing facilities Product development Market development Price/cost leadership	HR planning Talent management Skills development Targeted recruitment Retention policies Leadership development	Workforce composition Attrition rates Skills audit Outcome of recruitment campaigns Learning and development activity levels Outcome of leadership surveys
Business drivers	Innovation Maximize added value Productivity Customer service Quality Satisfy stakeholders – investors, shareholders, employees, elected representatives	Talent management Skills development Total reward management Performance management Develop high-performance working Enhance motivation, engagement and commitment Leadership development	Balanced scorecard data Added-value ratios (eg added value per employee, added value per £ of employment cost) Productivity ratios (eg sales revenue per employee, units produced or serviced per employee) Outcomes of general employee opinion survey and other surveys covering engagement and commitment, leadership, reward management and performance management Analysis of competence level assessments Analysis of performance management assessments Analysis of customer surveys Analysis of outcomes of total quality programmes ROI from training activities Internal promotion rate Succession planning coverage

this (an HR or people management practice), that (improved business results) will happen.' There is a choice of approach as summarized below:

∎ The employee–customer–profit chain links employee satisfaction to customer satisfaction to profitability (cf Rucci *et al*, 1998).

∎ The Nationwide Building Society Genome II human capital investment model quantifies the impact that employee commitment has on customer satisfaction and business performance. The model uses data from existing sources. It is possible to use data modelling to predict the impact that a change in one factor affecting employee commitment would have on customer satisfaction and ultimately on business performance (cf IRS, 2005).

∎ Business impact modelling (Mercer) predicts the outcome of specific people interventions and therefore anticipates the return on investment from a particular programme (cf Mathewman, 2006).

∎ ROI – the net income generated from expenditure on an HR process, eg training (cf Kearns, 2005b).

There are three difficulties to be overcome. The first is that these approaches, other than ROI, are hard to develop. The description by Suff (IRS, 2005a) of how the Nationwide Building Society built on the concept of the employee–customer–profit chain quoted Tony Houchen, Senior Manager, P&D Planning at Nationwide as saying: 'We were keen to target our investment in HR so that the return on investment could be maximised. Rather than a scatter-gun approach to allocating resources to HR areas such as reward and development, we wanted to prioritise our investment at the front end of the profit chain.' The two stages of the first project, Genome I, were first, an exploratory investigation to identify correlated data, and second, building mathematical models using the linear relationships between the data. The latter stage involved quantifying the strength of dependence between data items to predict the impact of change. Genome I was developed by ORC International who also conduct the Nationwide Building Society's employee opinion survey. Genome II was developed in-house.

The second difficulty is that these approaches, especially ROI, depend on a number of assumptions that cannot easily be supported by reliable evidence. It is difficult to prove direct causation, so many other factors creep in. But it can be argued that even so, the process of trying to establish causal links increases understanding of relationships between HR inputs and business outcomes and will therefore help to make decisions on HR priorities.

The third difficulty is that the first two approaches require the use of advanced statistical techniques such as the calculation of correlations, factor analysis, regression analysis and multi-variant analysis, which will require specialist skills not usually found in HR departments.

INFORMATION ON INTANGIBLE VALUE FOR THE INVESTMENT COMMUNITY

The demand from the investment community is growing for information to explain intangible value. Human capital being a large part of intangible value. Although opinion is divided on the extent of the demand and interest in human capital from investors and analysts. Gillen, writing in *Professional Investor* in March 2006, states: 'There is a growing awareness of the importance of non-financials in building the business case inside companies, a fact increasingly recognised by management team and investors.'

However, to the dismay of the HR profession the guidance developed by the Accounting Standards Board (2003) for implementing the now defunct OFR made very little mention of people data at all.

The evidence currently indicates that what the investment community is looking for is measures of performance at organizational level. However, very few companies are as yet in a position to provide these measures. We need to develop a greater understanding of what is required and what the HR role might be in putting this information together. The danger is that without this investors will fall back on accountancy models which, while providing hard financial measures, will not contain sufficient explanation to demonstrate the real contribution of human capital as a business driver.

CONVINCING SENIOR MANAGEMENT

A business case has to be made for HCM. It can be based on the proposition that human capital drives the business. This is difficult to deny, especially by those chief executives who still refer to people 'as our greatest asset'. But the case needs to be developed. It has to be demonstrated that HCM data and the analyses and evaluations that are derived from this data will provide guidance on business as well as HR strategy. Instances of how this will work need to be supplied. One example is the use of metrics to inform customer service strategies by identifying how improvements in levels of service can be achieved by such means as better selection, training and leadership, resulting in higher levels of engagement and skill and lower attrition rates.

The use of HCM as a basis for the preparation of realistic business cases justifying HR initiatives could also be mentioned. The focus has to be on the practical consequences of HCM in terms of the benefits to the business it will generate as measured by added value.

ENLISTING THE INTEREST AND INVOLVEMENT OF LINE MANAGEMENT

If frontline managers are going to be involved in making use of HCM metrics and evaluations, as they should be, the issues are how they are going to be convinced that it is worth their while and how are they going to be educated on the use they can make of HCM data.

One of the most important lessons learnt from the research conducted by Purcell and his colleagues (2003) at the University of Bath was that HR can initiate new policies and practices but it is the line that has the main responsibility for implementing them. In other words 'HR proposes but the line disposes.' If line managers are not disposed favourably towards what HR wants them to do they won't do it, or if compelled to, they will be half-hearted about it. As Purcell *et al* point out, high levels of organizational performance are not achieved simply by having a range of well-conceived HR policies and practices in place. What makes the difference is how these policies and practices are implemented. That is where the role of line managers in people management is crucial: 'The way line managers implement and enact policies, show leadership in dealing with employees and in exercising control come through as a major issue.' Purcell *et al* note that dealing with people is perhaps the aspect of their work in which line managers can exercise the greatest amount of discretion. If they use their discretion not to put HR's ideas into practice then the rhetoric is unlikely to be converted into reality. Performance management schemes often fail because of the reluctance of managers to carry out reviews. It is, as Purcell *et al* point out, line managers who bring HR policies to life.

Another factor affecting the role of line management is their ability to do the HR tasks assigned to them. People-centred activities such as defining roles, interviewing, reviewing performance, providing feedback, coaching and identifying learning and development needs all require special skills. Some managers have them: many don't. Performance-related pay schemes sometimes fail because of untrained line managers.

The growing use of 'self-service' for managers, ie dealing on-line themselves with a number of HR administrative tasks such as maintaining absenteeism and timekeeping records and updating personal information, is also a factor affecting the impact of HCM on them. They may have to be helped by HR to make better use of the data they have got.

The case for HCM for line managers should be based on the premises that they will be able to get better results through their people if they have data on how those people perform and on aspects of behaviour, such as absenteeism, that affect their performance. Line managers need to be convinced that the information will be readily available and will be useable as a means of indicating where actions within their area of discretion need to be taken.

It is essential to avoid presenting an overly complex version of HCM to them. It will only generate the response 'I've better things to do with my time.' Neil Roden, Group Director of HR at The Royal Bank of Scotland, renowned for its HCM, told *Personnel Today* (7 December, 2004) that getting managers involved in the process meant being careful not to overcomplicate things:

> When people start rolling out statistics and regression analysis, your eyes can glaze over a bit. This has its place but nowhere near line managers. What you need to say to line managers is: 'Would you like to know what your staff think about x, y and z? Would you like to know the connection between what that is and how you are doing as a business?' Even better, 'Would you like to know some of the things that if you fixed them would get you a bigger bonus because your business performance would be through the roof?' You need to do it in a language that businesses like and understand, and in ways they are used to so it doesn't seem as though it's from outer space.

CONVINCING HR SPECIALISTS

As Mayo (2006) has pointed out: 'Many HR professional are uncomfortable with the whole concept of more measurement. This may be philosophical – a belief that doing the right things is more important than trying to measure. Or it may be due to unease about how to go about the whole measuring process, and concern that any data may lack reliability or be misinterpreted.'

HR specialists will not need to be convinced that they should collect and use basic data such as attrition rates, absenteeism rates and analyses of workforce composition. However, following a number of recent discussions with practitioners, it is becoming clear that a large proportion do not believe that the more sophisticated applications of HCM are for them. They may recognize the need for more advanced and revealing measurements and appreciate that if these were available they would be in a stronger position to influence business strategy, produce business cases to justify HR initiatives and demonstrate the impact made by HR on business results, but they feel that HCM uses a number of esoteric and time-consuming techniques which they have neither the inclination, time or, perhaps, the skills to use.

To deal with this problem it is necessary to demonstrate the practical use of HCM – how it can help HR people not only to do their job better but also to convey to management that the HR function *is* doing it better in terms that senior managers understand – how it contributes to achieving better business results; the return on investment it generates. And the rhetoric emerging from commentators quoted at the beginning of this chapter is not enough. The reality of what can be done has to be proved by references to instances of what *has* been done. And although a number of examples of HCM's practical value have been given in this book, more are required, covering small- to medium-sized firms as well as the huge financial sector organizations with the resources available to develop advanced HCM practices.

STAGED DEVELOPMENT OF HCM

Convincing HR specialists of the value, relevance and feasibility of HCM is easier if they appreciate that they do not have to transform themselves overnight into high-powered statisticians. They can be helped to appreciate that HCM is not an all or nothing matter. It can be applied in stages as set out in Table 10.2.

Table 10.2 Stages in developing HCM

Stages	Data (internal – benchmarked where appropriate)	Applications
Basic 1 – readily available people data	Attrition Absenteeism/sickness Workforce composition (skills analysis) Grievances References to employment tribunals	Carry out trend analysis Carry out comparative analysis Report on performance to line managers Take remedial action (immediate and strategic): – attraction and retention policies – absence management policies – HR plans – employee relations policies
Basic 2 – HR quantitative performance data	Achievement of agreed service levels Response rates to requests for advice or services Time to fill vacancies Cost of recruitment Training days per employee Ratio of HR costs to total costs Ratio of HR staff to employees	Monitor performance of HR Identify areas for improvement Report to HR staff on performance
Intermediate 1 – employee opinion data	Employee questionnaire Engagement and commitment survey Reward survey Performance management survey	Identify and take action on general employee issues concerning commitment, engagement, motivation and morale Identify and take action on specific employee issues Report to line managers on performance Provide guidance to longer-term HR strategies
Intermediate 2 – employee performance data	Added value per employee Profit per employee Added value per £ of employment costs Performance management assessments	Carry out trend analysis Carry out comparative analysis Report on performance to management (and externally) Identify areas for remedial action Provide guide to business and HR strategy
Advanced	Measurement of impact of HR policies and practices on business performance ROI calculations on training and other HR activities	Guide the development of business and HR strategy Support business cases for HR initiatives

A complete HCM approach would embrace all these stages. But development could start with the basic analysis of available data and progress through the intermediate stage to the advanced stage. What we have is an elevator from the ground to the top that can be accessed at any floor. Some organizations plunge straight into the intermediate stage of obtaining and analysing employee opinion data on the grounds that this provides key information on the direction of HR strategy and the problems that have to be eradicated.

DEVELOPING THE HCM SKILLS OF HR SPECIALISTS

The future development of HCM depends on the existence of HR specialists who are not only interested in doing it but also have the skills required, as listed in Chapter 9. Syrett (2006) suggests that to get HCM to work: 'One or more senior HR practitioners will need training and/or extensive experience in basic survey/statistical methodology and empirical analysis.'

This does not apply so much to the basic stages as defined above. The level of skill required to collect, interpret, analyse and comment on data is no more than should be expected from anyone who is professionally qualified in HR. It is necessary at the intermediate stage to be familiar with survey techniques. But suppliers of diagnostic questionnaires such as Gallop, ORC International and Saratoga can provide the analytical expertise required, which is in any case not too difficult to learn. The skills used at the advanced stage to produce assessments of the impact of HR practices on business results are indeed outside the range of many practitioners who are not qualified statisticians familiar with such techniques as factor and multi-variant analysis or have not been trained in academic research techniques. Outside expertise may be necessary to develop the metrics as was the case in the Nationwide Building Society, although HR staff there acquired the skills when working alongside the consultants and now go it alone. The ability to produce return on investment assessments also requires skills that not all HR practitioners possess, but the skills can be learnt, especially if HR and finance are working as partners, as they should.

THE MEANING OF ADDED VALUE

The future of HCM depends on the extent to which it can provide the basis for achieving added value through people. HCM is sometimes described as a value-added approach to people management. This concept of added value looms large but is often used rhetorically as a symbol of what HCM is about. The real meaning of the phrase is somewhat obscure.

But before defining added value it is necessary to explore the meaning of value. HCM is about the value that people provide for organizations. It is founded on the belief that it is important to understand the factors that will create that value, and Mayo (2004) emphasizes that HR practitioners need to understand its meaning. One way of describing value is in terms of contribution. As defined by Brown and Armstrong (1999) 'contribution captures the full scope of what people do, the level of skill and competence they apply and the results they achieve, which all contribute to the organization achieving its long-term goals'. Contribution can be measured through performance management processes, especially the so-called mixed model, in which the two elements of contribution – results achieved and applied competencies – are assessed. Contribution-related pay, which is largely replacing performance-related pay, is founded on this approach – contingent pay decisions are based on assessments of both the outcomes of the work carried out by individuals and the inputs in terms of levels of competence and competency that have influenced these outcomes. It focuses on what people in organizations are there to do, that is, to contribute by their skill and efforts to the achievement of the purpose of their organization or team. This is very much in accord with the philosophy of HCM.

When we turn to the concept of added value we have to start with its technical meaning in accounts where added value is defined as the value added to the cost of raw materials and bought-out parts by the process of production and distribution. To calculate it, the cost of bought-in items are deducted from the turnover figure that appears in the profit and loss account to give a figure of the value added by the efforts of the company's employees to make the best – most productive – use of the capital and other resources available to them. For employees in particular the value-added statements that appear in company reports focus on their contribution. When expressed as value added per employee the statements provide probably the best method available of attaching value to what employees do.

Saratoga (2005) uses an added value metric called the Human Capital ROI as one of the key performance indicators. This takes pre-tax profit generated for each unit of currency invested in remuneration costs. The resultant ratio indicates how many units of currency (pounds, euros or dollars) are produced for each unit of currency paid to an employee. The human capital index in Europe in 2002 was €1.07.

In non-accounting terms, added value represents the contribution made by employees to business success. An increase in added value indicates that employees are contributing more. The rhetoric attached to the phrase in HCM-speak simply means obtaining a higher return (increased profitability or productivity) from investing in people. The aim is to ensure that the value of the contribution of people exceeds the cost of generating it. It also means that any HR initiative should be judged against the criteria of added value – to what extent can it be justified because the extent to which it enhances performance exceeds the cost of introducing it.

WHAT IS MEANT BY REGARDING PEOPLE AS ASSETS

Many commentators such as Kearns (2005a) and Mayo (2001) contend that the defining characteristic of HCM is that it regards employees as assets rather than costs (although in 2006 Mayo commented that: 'people are always accounted for as costs, and never as investments, whereas in truth they could be either'). This, they say, distinguishes HCM from HRM as the latter persists in treating employees as costs. As explained in Chapter 2, this latter statement is misleading – the emphasis on employees as assets is shared by both HCM and the full version of HRM.

But it is not universally accepted that employees should be seen simply as assets. As Donkin (2005) comments:

> Books and reports in human capital management have tended to persist with the concept of the employee as an asset. This is one way of looking at the workplace. But it can be unhelpful since it ignores the cost of employees and fails to illustrate that employees can be valued in different ways. One example is the contracted professional soccer player.

Another issue concerning the valuation of people as assets is that, unlike other assets in a firm, human capital is not owned by the organization but exists because of the employment relationship.

It is maintained by Davenport (1999) that the concept of regarding people as assets is limited, indeed questionable, because:

▌ Workers should not be treated as passive assets to be bought, sold and replaced at the whim of their owners – increasingly, they actively control their own working lives.

▌ The notion that companies own human assets as they own machines is unacceptable in principle and inapplicable in practice; it short-changes people by placing them in the same category as plant and equipment.

▌ No system of 'human asset accounting' has succeeded in producing a convincing method of attaching financial values to human resources. In any case, this demeans the more intangible added value that can be delivered to organizations by people.

However, treating employees as assets focuses attention on a fundamental aim of people management – that the organization obtains and retains the skilled, committed and well-motivated workforce it needs. This means taking steps to assess and satisfy future people requirements and to enhance and develop the inherent capacities of people – their contributions, potential and employability – by providing learning and continuous development opportunities. It involves the operation of 'rigorous recruitment and selection procedures, performance-contingent incentive compensation systems, and management development and training activities linked to the needs of the business' (Becker *et al*, 1997). It also means engaging in talent management – the process of acquiring and nurturing talent, wherever it is and wherever it is needed, by using a number of interdependent HRM policies and practices in the fields of resourcing, learning and development, performance management and succession planning.

SELECTING THE MEASURES

The future of HCM it is not entirely dependent on selecting the best measures – it is what is done with them that will count. Measures have indeed a crucial part to play but only if those selected provide guidance on or support for future action. Information should be capable of year-on-year comparison thus enabling trends to be identified. The aim should be to identify quantifiable data, but when this is impossible a qualitative approach can be justified as long as it clearly identifies what is happening, why it is happening and what conclusions can be drawn from the analysis to evaluate performance or guide future developments.

It is often suggested that the starting point should be to use data that is readily available. But this approach begs the question as to whether the data would be any use. As Neely (1998) has commented, the tendency is to measure what is easy to measure rather than what is relevant. Syrett (2006) emphasizes that: 'The acid test of effective measurement is the process by which it is translated into actionable policies and plans... the right data is useless if it is not acted upon.'

The first question to be asked when introducing HCM is indeed: 'What data have we got?' But if a full approach to HCM is contemplated, it is necessary to answer the follow-up questions: 'What data do we need?', 'Is the data available?' 'How are we going to get that data?', and 'How are we going to use that data?' There may be problems in extracting the information and its value may not justify the effort involved. There is a huge choice of measures and it will be necessary to ensure that the number selected is manageable. It is far better to select a relatively small number of measures directly relevant to the key business drivers of the organization rather than indiscriminately adopting any metric that happens to be available. The aim should be to keep it simple.

ANALYSING AND EVALUATING THE DATA

The future of HCM as an effective HRM tool does not rest simply on identifying the data required and then collecting it. The processes of analysing and evaluating the data are what matter. Data analysis means looking at trends, not just actuals, as well as benchmarking. The aim of the analysis is to draw out from what may be a mass of data the information that will inform action and then to present that information in a way that clarifies the issues. The data must be submitted to critical evaluation (see page 38).

THE FUTURE OF EXTERNAL REPORTING

As noted in Chapter 6, the requirements for external reporting have had a chequered history over the last few years. The recommendations made by The Accounting for People Task Force (2003) stated that: 'Reporting on HCM to external stakeholders should have the effect of driving real improvements that will feed into corporate performance.' The Task Force recommended a number of general principles, perhaps the most important of these being: 'Reports on HCM should have a strategic focus, be balanced and objective, and based on sound data.' It was recognized that measures have to be relevant to the particular drivers of each business – no attempt was made to indicate what measures might be included in reports.

Also in 2003 the Accounting Standards Board produced its preliminary statement on what should be contained in the Operating and Financial Review (OFR) as part of a company's annual report. The government produced draft regulations on the OFR in 2004 and at the same time a working group on the OFR set up by the government published guidelines on complying with the regulations (DTI, 2004). These included 16 principles, of which several dealt explicitly or implicitly with human capital issues. The following example was given by the group: 'A service business with few physical assets... and depending for its source of competitive advantage on the supply of particular human skills, will plan over a period consistent with its ability to recruit, train and develop its key resource.'

The Accounting Standards Board released an exposure draft on the OFR later that year, which argued against a generic approach to measurement, and wanted company directors to develop the measures appropriate to their business. This is in keeping with the view of the Accounting Standards Board that the OFR should be a report on the company as seen through the eyes of management.

However, after all this activity, the Chancellor of the Exchequer unexpectedly announced in November 2005 that the government was abolishing the requirement for the OFR. Instead, organizations would be expected to produce a Business Review, which is part of the requirements of the European Accounts Modernisation Directive. Like the OFR, the Business Review requires:

- a balanced and comprehensive analysis of the development and performance of the company in the financial year;

- a description of the principal risks and uncertainties facing the company;

- analysis using appropriate financial and non-financial performance indicators including environmental and employee issues.

The requirements for the Business Review refer to the need for human capital data but it leaves it largely up to managers to decide how to do this and what information to include.

What may emerge from any forthcoming debate on the human capital components of the Business Review is a statement of possible headings along the lines originally developed by the CIPD (2003), namely:

∎ the profile of the workforce and its diversity;

∎ senior executive remuneration;

∎ the quality of leadership and management strength;

∎ how well labour costs have been managed over time;

∎ evidence of a coherent, robust people strategy that is mapped to the stated business strategy for the next three years;

∎ evidence that current people management practice (especially regarding acquisition, motivation and retention) are improving organizational and business performance;

∎ current and forecasted returns on people investment in the next three to five years;

∎ the value of human capital assets and future investments, especially in major corporate decisions such as mergers and acquisitions;

∎ comparator listings in financial league tables – such as industry FTSE or analyst ratings;

∎ position in 'best company to work for' surveys.

But these will not be mandatory.

Meanwhile, as reported in *People Management* July 2006, Investors in People has set up a think-tank to explore a set of universal principles for comparing companies' human capital. How universal these principles will be remains to be seen. They may, however, refer to the sort of headings listed above and add some views on possible generally accepted ratios such as added value per employee.

CONCLUSIONS

The future of HCM depends on appreciating the issues discussed above and acting accordingly. In developing HCM what we need to remember is its fundamental purpose, which is to achieve a better understanding of what *is* going on so as to be in a better position to decide what *should* go on.

Ultimately, HCM is there to achieve the aim that was summarized by one human capital specialist as follows: 'to look at how the business performs through our people'. The emphasis is on performance. Not just measuring and analysing it but doing something about it.

Appendix

The HCM toolkit

PURPOSE OF THE TOOLKIT

The purpose of the toolkit is to provide guidance on introducing and operating HCM processes within an organization. It is designed to help you to answer the following questions:

- What is an HCM approach?
- Do we need to adopt one?
- If so, how do we do it?
- How do we introduce HCM?
- How do we operate HCM?

WHAT IS AN HCM APPROACH?

An HCM approach starts with an appreciation of the meaning and importance of human capital. It is based on the belief that the process of measuring key aspects of the ways in which human capital is developed and managed, and of assessing the impact it makes on organizational performance, ie HCM, will guide managements on what needs to be done to obtain added value from people and improve business results.

The meaning of human capital

Human capital is the knowledge, skills, abilities and capacity to develop and innovate possessed by people in an organization. It is an aspect of intellectual capital – the stocks and flows of knowledge available to an organization, and is associated with the concepts of social capital – the knowledge derived from relationships within and outside the organization, and organizational capital – the institutionalized knowledge possessed by an organization and stored in databases, manuals, etc.

The importance of HCM

HCM is important because it enables organizations to make more productive use of people through measurements, analysis and evaluation rather than guesswork. It provides guidance on the development of HR and business strategies that enable improvements in levels of business performance, and higher levels of engagement to be achieved by such means as better selection, training and leadership. It encourages the initiation of processes for the assessment and satisfaction of future people requirements. It provides the basis for developing policies and practices that enhance the inherent capacities of people – their contributions, potential and employability – by providing learning and continuous development opportunities.

The process of HCM

The process of HCM is illustrated in Figure A.1.

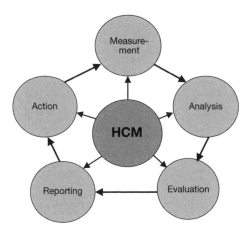

Figure A.1   The process of HCM

DO WE NEED TO ADOPT AN HCM APPROACH?

To assist in deciding whether or not an HCM approach is needed and if so, whether you are ready for it, look at the following 10 statements in Questionnaire 1 and decide on the extent to which you agree or disagree with each one and why, referring to related questions as appropriate.

Questionnaire 1: Do we need to adopt a HCM approach?

Statement 1 I like the idea of HCM but believe that the effort required to introduce it would not be worthwhile.

If you agree to any extent with this statement you need to consider your answers to the succeeding statements in this section and the remaining contents of this toolkit. This might convince you that (a) HCM is worth the effort and that (b) if you want, you could stage its introduction, starting with basic data. You should also consider the reasons why you believe this to be true.

Statement 2 I am satisfied that we have all the data required to measure the effectiveness and impact of HR policies and that we use it productively.

Statement 3 I am convinced that we do not need to do anything more with our data than we already do.

If you fully or partly agree with statements 2 and 3 then that could be an end to it, but it would still be useful to run through the remaining questions and the rest of the toolkit to find out if there are arguments which would help to change your mind. It would also be helpful to review the data you currently generate and use, maybe in the light of the review of data in this book, to make sure there are no other forms of data available to you which could enhance your understanding of the contribution of human capital.

Now consider the following statements asking yourself the questions underneath each.

Statement 4 Top management would appreciate more information on the effectiveness and impact on the business of HR policies and practices.

▌ Is there an expressed demand?

▌ Have decisions been made which would have benefited from more information on human capital?

▌ Do top managers understanding the contribution of HR to the business?

Statement 5 Line managers would benefit from having more information on how effective they are as people managers.

▌ Have they asked for information you cannot provide?

▌ Do they fully understanding their role as implementers of HR practice?

▌ Do they understand the impact of their behaviour on the performance of others and hence business performance?

Statement 6 HCM would provide me with invaluable data to support any business case I would want to make for an HR initiative.

▌ Can you justify this with HCM data?

Statement 7 HCM is essential as a guide to the development of HR and business strategy.

▌ What is the role of HR in the development of business strategy?

▌ How would this role change if more HCM information were available?

Statement 8 HCM would provide invaluable information to me and my colleagues on the effectiveness of the HR function.

▌ How do you currently demonstrate effectiveness of the function?

▌ How is HR perceived in the organization?

▌ If you could effectively demonstrate the contribution of human capital how would this affect the perception of HR and its effectiveness?

Statement 9 HCM is essential as a means of generating meaningful information on human capital issues for the Business Review.

▌ Can you already supply the information that will be needed to comply with the Business Review?

If the answers to these questions are mainly encouraging you are ready for HCM and willing to put in the work required as suggested in this toolkit. However, your answers may indicate priorities. You might, for example, be particularly concerned with providing data for line managers and HR staff and you might, at this stage at least, be less concerned about external reporting. You also need to consider the skills required to develop HCM (statement 10).

Statement 10 I or my colleagues have all the skills necessary to develop HCM.

▌ Can you access sufficient statistical skill to collect and analyse the data?

▌ Are you able to understand what you need to measure to identify the key business drivers and develop HCM that is relevant for your organization?

If you feel that there is a good case for HCM but do not fully agree with statement 9 then you will need to assess the existing level of knowledge and skills possessed by you and your colleagues and establish the gap between the existing and required skills and what needs to be done to fill that gap (see Questionnaire 20, page 199).

HOW DO WE ADOPT AN HCM APPROACH?

If a good case has been established, three questions need to be answered in considering how an HCM approach should be adopted:

▌ What use are we going to make of HCM? – see Questionnaire 2.

▌ How do we make the case to management? – see Questionnaire 3.

▌ How are we going to introduce HCM? – see Questionnaire 4.

Questionnaire 2: What use are we going to make of HCM?

What are the possible uses of HCM?	Which of these uses are we going to adopt and why?	What is the preferred timescale for introducing this aspect of HCM?	If applicable, why don't we want to adopt this use?

• Identify the need for remedial action
• Take immediate or longer-term action:
 	
  – attraction and retention policies
  – absence management policies
  – HR plans
  – employee relations policies
  – other HR policies
 	
• Report to line managers on their performance as people managers			

• Monitor the performance of HR • Identify areas for improvement • Report to HR staff on their performance			
• Identify and take action on general employee issues concerning commitment, engagement, motivation and morale • Identify and take action on specific employee issues • Report to line managers on their performance • Provide a guide to longer-term HR strategies			
• Report on performance to management • Identify areas for remedial action • Provide a guide to business and HR strategy			
• Produce external reports (Business Review)			
• Identify the impact of HR policies and practices on business performance • Guide the development of business and HR strategy • Support business cases for HR initiatives			

Questionnaire 3: How do we make the business case for HCM to management?

This questionnaire sets out a number of general arguments for HCM against which specific benefits to the organization can be assessed.

General arguments in favour of HCM	Degree of relevance to the organization (high, moderate, low)	Specific benefits to the organization
Develop an understanding of what translates human capital into business value as a basis for developing realistic HR and business strategies		
Establish a clear line of sight between HR interventions and business success (Kearns, 2005a)		
Demonstrate that HR practices produce value for money in terms, for example, of ROI		
Provide data for internal reports that identify areas for improvement in HR practice		
Provide data for internal reports that indicate levels of people performance in the organization and identify areas for improvement		
Provide data for internal reports on the effectiveness of line managers as people managers		
Provide data for internal reports on the effectiveness of the HR function and identify areas for improvement		
Provide information on the value of the organization's human capital		
Provide data for external reports (eg the Business Review) that demonstrate that the organization is implementing innovative and productive policies to enhance the value obtained from its human capital		

Questionnaire 4: How are we going to introduce HCM?

This questionnaire sets out the general points to consider when contemplating the introduction of HCM. The business case point was dealt with in Questionnaire 3. The remaining points are covered in the next two sections of this toolkit.

What points do we need to cover?	How are we going to deal with them?
How do we make the business case for HCM to management?	
How do we brief line managers and employees generally on the purpose and use of HCM and how it affects them?	
How do we train line managers on the use they can make for HCM?	
How do we stage the introduction of HCM?	
What data do we need?	
How do we collect the data?	
How do we ensure that HR has the HCM skills it needs?	
What internal reports should we produce?	
What information are we going to provide for external reports?	
How are we going to use HCM data as a basis for developing HR strategy?	
How will HCM influence business strategy?	

INTRODUCING HCM

The programme for introducing HCM is illustrated in Figure A.2. The elements of the programme are dealt with in the rest of this toolkit.

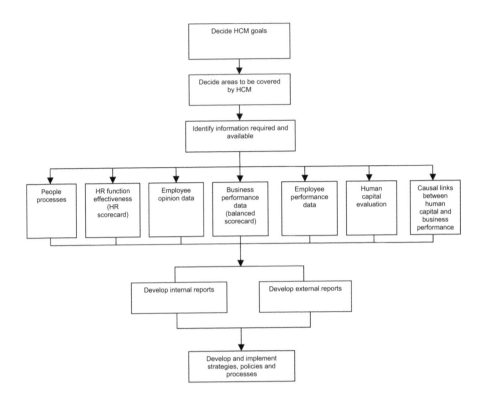

Figure A.2 Programme for introducing HCM

DECIDE HCM GOALS

It is necessary to understand what you are setting out to do with HCM. Questionnaire 5 covers a preliminary analysis of the drivers that will affect goals and Questionnaire 6 will help to clarify your aims by assessing the importance of different goals and the extent to which the present arrangements are effective.

Questionnaire 5: HCM drivers

Possible drivers	Extent to which relevant and why
The need to achieve specified strategic goals	
The recognition that these goals can only be attained by the effective use of resources and that the key resource is people, whose knowledge, skills and abilities create value and produce human capital and therefore competitive advantage	
An appreciation of the importance of understanding the factors that will create value through people	
The realization that to understand and apply these factors it is necessary to measure and assess the actual or potential impact of HR processes and to base HR and business strategy on the outcomes of these measurements	
The need to ensure that HR processes provide value for money	
Other	

Questionnaire 6: HCM goals

This questionnaire could usefully be completed jointly by HR and senior and line management.

Goal	Importance*	Effectiveness*
Obtain, analyse and report on data that informs the direction of HR strategies and processes		
Inform the development of business strategy		
Use measurements to prove that superior HRM strategies and processes deliver superior results		
Reinforce the belief that HRM strategies and processes create value through people		
Determine the impact of people on business results		
Assess the value of the organization's human capital		
Improve the effectiveness of HR		
Improve the effectiveness of line managers as people managers		
Provide data on the performance of the organization's human capital for external reports, eg the Business Review		
Demonstrate that HR processes provide value for money in terms of return on capital employed		

* Scale: 10 = high, 0 = low

DECIDE AREAS TO BE COVERED BY HCM

Use Questionnaire 7 to decide on the priority to be given to developing different aspects of HCM.

Questionnaire 7: HCM priorities

HCM area	Priority*	Introduce by:
Make better use of existing people process data		
Develop improved people process data		
Obtain and use better quantitative data on the performance of HR		
Develop an HR scorecard		
Obtain and use data on the people management performance of line managers		
Develop a balanced scorecard		
Conduct employee opinion surveys		
Calculate ROI in training		
Calculate impact of HR policies and practices on business performance		
Estimate the value of human capital		

Scale: 10 = highest priority; 0 = no priority

IDENTIFY MEASURES REQUIRED AND AVAILABLE

The general factors that determine the selection of measures are:

▌ The type of organization – measures are context dependent.

▌ The business goals of the organization.

▌ The business drivers of the organization, ie the factors that contribute to the achievement of business goals, especially those that involve the acquisition, retention, development and motivation of people so that the expertise and skills required are available. Business drivers include such matters as innovation, expansion through mergers and acquisitions, product development, market development, increases in revenue, price leadership, control of costs, customer service and quality.

▌ The existing key performance indicators used in the organization.

▌ The existence of a balanced scorecard approach, the quadrants used and the elements within each quadrant.

▌ The availability of data.

▌ The use of data – measures should only be selected that can be put to good use in guiding strategy and reporting on performance.

▌ The manageability of data – there may be a wide choice of metrics and it is essential to be selective in the light of the above analysis so that the burden of collecting, analysing and evaluating the data is not too great and people do not suffer from information overload. Remember that the cost of perfection is prohibitive, the cost of sensible approximation is less – the aim should be to keep it simple.

Questionnaires 8 (people data and processes), 9 (HR function effectiveness) 10 (causal links) and 11 (human capital evaluation) provide a framework for analysing requirements and availability. Note that where appropriate the data should include actuals, ratios and trends.

Questionnaire 8: Analysis of measures requirements – people data and processes

Measures – people data and processes	Possible use – analysis leading to action	Required ✓	Available now ✓	To be made available ✓
Workforce composition– gender, race, age, full-time staff, part-time staff	Analyse the extent of diversity Assess the implications of a preponderance of employees in different age groups, eg extent of loss through retirement Assess the extent to which the organization is relying on part-time staff			

Measures – people data and processes	Possible use – analysis leading to action	Required ✓	Available now ✓	To be made available ✓
Length of service distribution	Indicate the level of success in retaining employees Indicate the preponderance of long- or short-serving employees Enable analyses of the performance of more experienced employees to be assessed			
Skills analysis/ assessment – graduates, professionally/ technically qualified, skilled workers	Assess skill levels against requirements Indicate areas where steps have to be taken to deal with shortfalls			
Attrition – employee turnover rates for different categories of management and employees	Indicate areas where steps have to be taken to increase retention rates Provide a basis for assessing levels of commitment			
Attrition – cost of	Support the business case for taking steps to reduce attrition			
Absenteeism/sickness rates	Identify problems and the need for more effective attendance management policies			
Average number of vacancies as a percentage of total workforce	Identify potential shortfall problem areas			
Cost per recruit	Control the use of different sources			

Measures – people data and processes	Possible use – analysis leading to action	Required ✓	Available now ✓	To be made available ✓
Ratio of acceptances to job offers	Attractiveness of the organization			
Total payroll costs (pay and benefits)	Provide data for productivity analysis			
Compa-ratio – actual rates of pay as a percentage of policy rates	Enable control to be exercised over management of the pay structure			
Percentage of employees in different categories of contingent pay or payment-by-result schemes	Demonstrate the extent to which the organization believes that pay should be related to contribution			
Total pay review increases for different categories of employees as a percentage of pay	Compare actual with budgeted payroll increase costs Benchmark pay increases			
Average bonuses or contingent pay awards as a percentage of base pay for different categories of managers and employees	Analyse the cost of contingent pay Compare actual and budgeted increases Benchmark increases			
Outcome of equal pay reviews	Reveal the pay gap between male and female employees			
Personal development plans completed as a percentage of employees	Indicate the level of learning and development activity			

Measures – people data and processes	Possible use – analysis leading to action	Required ✓	Available now ✓	To be made available ✓
Training hours per employee	Indicate the amount (not quality) of training activity			
Percentage of managers taking part in formal management development programmes	Indicate the level of learning and development activity			
Internal promotion rate (percentage of promotions filled from within)	Indicate the extent to which talent management programmes are successful			
Succession planning coverage (percentage of managerial jobs for which successors have been identified)	Indicate the extent to which talent management programmes are successful			
Percentage of employees taking part in formal performance reviews	Indicate the level of performance management activity			
Distribution of performance ratings by category of staff and department	Indicate inconsistencies, questionable distributions and trends in assessments			
Accident severity and frequency rates	Assess health and safety programmes			
Cost savings/revenue increases resulting from employee suggestion schemes	Measure the value created by employees			

Questionnaire 9: Analysis of measures requirements – HR function effectiveness

HCM is not just about assessing the effectiveness of HR, the levels of HR competency and service delivery achieved by the function can make a major impact on the availability, use and contribution of an organization's human capital and can therefore usefully be included in an HCM programme. This questionnaire provides a framework for analysing what measures may be required.

Measures – HR function effectiveness	Possible use – analysis leading to action	Required ✓	Available now ✓	To be made available ✓
Achievement of agreed service delivery levels: – time to fill vacancies – response rates to requests for services or advice – provision of required information – provision of required training – provision of advice on employment law issues – handling grievances and employee concerns – handling industrial relations issues	Identify strengths and weaknesses and areas for development or improvement			
Outcomes of employee opinion surveys	Assess the impact of HR policies and practices on motivation, engagement and commitment			
Attrition levels	Assess the effectiveness of HR's recruitment, induction and reward policies and processes			

Measures – HR function effectiveness	Possible use – analysis leading to action	Required ✓	Available now ✓	To be made available ✓
Absenteeism	Assess the effectiveness of HR's absence management policy and process			
Grievances	Assess the effectiveness of HR's grievance handling policy and process			
Ratio of HR costs to total costs	Assess the cost effectiveness of HR			
Cost of recruitment	Exercise control over HR costs			
Cost of outsourcing				
Cost of using consultants				
Ratio of HR staff to total number of employees	Exercise control over HR staffing levels Benchmark with other comparable organizations			
HR scorecard: *HR competencies* – administrative expertise, employee advocacy, strategy execution and change agency *HR practices* – communication, work design, selection, development, measurement and rewards *HR systems* – alignment, integration and differentiation *HR deliverables* – workforce mindset, technical knowledge, and workforce behaviour	Overall assessment of the performance of the HR function			

Questionnaire 10: Use of employee opinion surveys

Data obtained from employee opinion surveys provide one of the most important means of measuring the effectiveness of HR policies in terms of the reactions of people to them and therefore indicating where improvements are required. This questionnaire covers the use and choice of surveys.

Question on use of employee opinion surveys	Response ✓		Additional questions/comments
	Yes	No	
Do you use any form of employee opinion survey?			If 'yes', what are your objectives?
			If 'no', do you intend to use one and if so why?
If you use one or more opinion surveys, is it one or any of the following?:			How often do you conduct surveys?
			Who is covered?
– ORC international employee opinion survey			What response rate did you get for your last survey?
– Saratoga engagement and commitment matrix			
– Gallop engagement survey			Are you satisfied with that response rate? If not, what are you doing about it?
– IES engagement survey			
– CIPD people and performance employee questionnaire			
– CIPD people and performance climate survey			
– Any other (specify)			
How do you administer/use the survey?			
– Report to top management setting out findings and implications			
– Full results communicated to all in writing or via intranet			
– Summarized results communicated to all in writing or by intranet			
– Communicate through briefing meetings with employees			
– Involve employees in discussing implications of survey			

Question on use of employee opinion surveys	Response ✓		Additional questions/comments
	Yes	No	
– Communicate findings to line managers – Involve line managers in discussing implications of the survey – As a major input to HR strategy and policy planning – To identify problems as a basis for taking steps to remedy them – As part of the external Business Report			Employee opinion surveys are only valuable to the extent that: – the results are communicated to all employees – employees have the opportunity to comment on them – senior managers are fully aware of the findings and their implications – use is made of the findings to guide the formulation of HR strategies and policies – steps are taken to remedy problems revealed by the survey

Examples of survey questionnaires that can be adopted or modified follow. These consist of a general opinion survey (Questionnaire 11), a survey focusing on engagement and commitment (Questionnaire 12) a leadership survey (Questionnaire 13) and two specialized surveys (Questionnaires 14 and 15) dealing respectively with reward and performance management. Note, however, that the advantage of using a 'proprietary' survey such as Gallop, ORC or Saratoga, apart from their expertise and the ease of administration, is that benchmarking data is available.

Questionnaire 11: General employee opinion survey

Please circle the number that most closely matches your opinion

1 = Strongly agree; 2 = Strongly disagree; 3 = Agree; 4 = Disagree

The organization				
I am proud to work for this organization	1	2	3	4
I would not encourage anyone else to work here	1	2	3	4
I want to go on working for this organization	1	2	3	4
Your job				
I like my job	1	2	3	4
I am not clear about what I am expected to achieve	1	2	3	4

I have plenty of scope to decide how to do my work	1	2	3	4
I have to work too hard to achieve the results expected of me	1	2	3	4
I am well motivated to do a good job	1	2	3	4
The balance between my work and domestic life is unsatisfactory	1	2	3	4

Your boss

My boss does a very good job	1	2	3	4
My boss gives me clear direction	1	2	3	4
My boss lets me know how I am getting on	1	2	3	4
My boss does not support me very well	1	2	3	4
My boss helps me to improve my performance	1	2	3	4
My boss treats everyone fairly	1	2	3	4

Learning and development

I have been given every opportunity to develop my knowledge and skills	1	2	3	4
I am satisfied with the career opportunities provided by the organization	1	2	3	4
I am not given much opportunity to discuss my development needs with my boss	1	2	3	4

Your pay

I am fairly paid for the work I do	1	2	3	4
I feel that my pay does not reflect my contribution	1	2	3	4
My pay compares favourably with what I could get elsewhere	1	2	3	4

Communication

I do not feel that I am fully informed about what the organization is setting out to do	1	2	3	4
I am told about the plans for my department/group	1	2	3	4

Teamwork and colleagues

The members of my team work very effectively together	1	2	3	4
I get on well with my colleagues	1	2	3	4

Questionnaire 12: Employee engagement and commitment survey

Please circle the number that most closely matches your opinion

1 = Strongly agree; 2 = Strongly disagree; 3 = Agree; 4 = Disagree

Engagement

I am very satisfied with the work I do	1	2	3	4
My job is interesting	1	2	3	4
I know exactly what I am expected to do	1	2	3	4
I am prepared to put myself out to do my work	1	2	3	4
My job is not very challenging	1	2	3	4
I am given plenty of freedom to decide how to do my work	1	2	3	4
I get plenty of opportunities to learn in this job	1	2	3	4
The facilities/equipment/tools provided are excellent	1	2	3	4
I do not get adequate support from my boss	1	2	3	4
My contribution is fully recognized	1	2	3	4
The experience I am getting now will be a great help in advancing my future career	1	2	3	4
I find it difficult to keep up with the demands of my job	1	2	3	4
I have no problems in achieving a balance between my work and my private life	1	2	3	4
I like working for my boss	1	2	3	4
I get on well with my work colleagues	1	2	3	4

Commitment

I think this organization is a great place in which to work	1	2	3	4
I believe I have a good future in this organization	1	2	3	4
I intend to go on working for this organization	1	2	3	4
I am not happy about the values of this organization – the ways in which it conducts its business	1	2	3	4
I believe that the products/services provided by this organization are excellent	1	2	3	4

Questionnaire 13: Leadership survey

Please circle the number that most closely matches your opinion

1 = Strongly agree; 2 = Strongly disagree; 3 = Agree; 4 = Disagree

I admire my boss	1	2	3	4
My boss clearly knows what he or she is doing	1	2	3	4
My boss is an effective leader	1	2	3	4
I am not confident in the ability of my boss to do his or her job	1	2	3	4
My boss gets the best out of his or her team	1	2	3	4
My boss encourages me to use my own initiative	1	2	3	4
My boss inspires me to do my best	1	2	3	4
I am given insufficient scope by my boss to do my job	1	2	3	4
My boss is decisive	1	2	3	4
I am not clear what my boss expects me to do	1	2	3	4
My boss gives me the support I need to do a good job	1	2	3	4
My boss regularly discusses with me how well I am doing my job	1	2	3	4
I get the guidance and coaching I need from my boss to develop my knowledge and skills	1	2	3	4
I do not get adequate feedback from my boss on my performance	1	2	3	4
My boss sets clear performance targets and standards	1	2	3	4
My boss values the opinions of me and my colleagues	1	2	3	4
My boss does not recognize my achievements	1	2	3	4
My boss is open to new ideas	1	2	3	4
My boss keeps his or her team fully informed of departmental plans	1	2	3	4
My boss deals sympathetically with any problems I have with achieving a balance between my work and my private life	1	2	3	4

Questionnaire 14: Reward survey

Please circle the number that most closely matches your opinion

1 = Strongly agree; 2 = Strongly disagree; 3 = Agree; 4 = Disagree

My contribution is adequately rewarded	1	2	3	4
Pay increases are handled fairly	1	2	3	4
I feel that my pay does not reflect my performance	1	2	3	4
My pay compares favourably with what I could get elsewhere	1	2	3	4
I am not paid fairly in comparison with other people doing similar work in the organization	1	2	3	4
I think the organization's pay policy is overdue for a review	1	2	3	4
Grading decisions are made fairly	1	2	3	4
I am not clear how decisions about my pay are made	1	2	3	4
I understand how my job has been graded	1	2	3	4
I get good feedback on my performance	1	2	3	4
I am clear about what I am expected to achieve	1	2	3	4
I like my job	1	2	3	4
The performance pay scheme encourages better performance	1	2	3	4
I am proud to work for the organization	1	2	3	4
I understand how my pay can progress	1	2	3	4
The job evaluation scheme works fairly	1	2	3	4
The benefits package compares well with those in other organizations	1	2	3	4
I would like more choice about the benefits I receive	1	2	3	4
I feel motivated after my performance review meeting	1	2	3	4
I do not understand the pay policies of the organization	1	2	3	4

Questionnaire 15: Performance management survey

Please indicate how you felt about performance management by recording your reactions to the following statements. State:

'A' if you fully agree   'B' if you partly agree   'C' if you disagree

I am quite satisfied that the objectives I agreed were fair
I felt that the meeting to agree objectives and standards of performance helped me to focus on what I should be aiming to achieve
I received good feedback from my manager on how I was doing
My manager was always prepared to provide guidance when I ran into problems at work
The performance review meeting was conducted by my manager in a friendly and helpful way
My manager fully recognized my achievements during the year
If any criticisms were made during the review meeting, they were acceptable because they were based on fact, not opinion
I was given plenty of opportunity by my manager to discuss the reasons for any of my work problems
I felt generally that the comments made by my manager at the meeting were fair
I felt motivated after the meeting
The meeting ended with a clear plan of action for the future with which I agreed
The action I have taken since the meeting has led to a distinct improvement in my performance

Business performance data

HCM is concerned with the impact of HR practices on business performance and it is therefore necessary to be aware of the business performance data available in order to establish links between them and HR practices.

Financial and operational data will include added value, profit, revenue, costs, customer opinion survey data and units produced or serviced. Overall performance data can be provided by the balanced scorecard. The standard quadrants (which can be varied) are financial, customer, internal business process, and learning and growth. There is no identified human capital dimension. But evidence of the contribution that people make can be found in all four of these quadrants using whatever measures have been adopted.

Employee performance data

Employee performance data provides information on the added value generated by employees and on their productivity. It can be used to report on performance to management and externally, to identify areas for remedial action and to provide guidance on the development of HR and business strategy. Questionnaire 16 lists the main measures that can be made available.

Questionnaire 16: Employee performance measures

Measures – employee performance data	Required	Available now	To be made available
Added value per employee			
Added value per £ of employment costs			
Pre-tax profit per employee			
Pre-tax profit per £ of employment costs			
Sales revenue per employee			
Sales revenue per £ of employment costs			
Units produced or serviced per employee			

Human capital evaluation

Human capital evaluation is the process of calculating the value of the people in an organization as assets. It is necessary to establish that this is a useful thing to do by completing Questionnaire 17 and, if so, then to consider the alternative ways of doing it.

Questionnaire 17: Reasons for evaluating human capital

Reason for valuing human capital	Extent of agreement		
	Fully agree	Limited agreement	Disagree
Human capital constitutes a key element of the market value of a company and as such needs to be valued to obtain a full understanding of what the company is worth and guide business planning			
A better understanding will be obtained of the value drivers in the company			
People in organizations add value and this needs to be measured to provide a basis for HR planning and for monitoring the effectiveness and impact of HR policies and practices			

Reason for valuing human capital	Extent of agreement		
	Fully agree	**Limited agreement**	**Disagree**
It will focus attention on what needs to be done to find, keep, develop and make the best use of the organization's human capital			
Measurements can be used to monitor progress in achieving strategic HR goals			
Provide critical data to investors when selecting and monitoring their company shares (Lees, 2004)			
'Without a more robust understanding of the nature, distribution and value of their employees' human capital, firms risk losing or downgrading that which they already have' (Scarborough and Elias, 2002)			

It may be agreed that human capital evaluation is a good thing but before proceeding to look at ways of doing it, the problems involved need to be considered. These are:

▌ The inherent difficulties of measuring the value of human capital – in the words of Scarborough and Elias (2002): 'Human capital is to a large extent non-standardised, tacit, dynamic, context dependent and embodied in people.'

▌ Any attempt at measurement requires the deployment of huge and largely unsupportable assumptions.

▌ There is no generally accepted accounting measure of human capital – companies generally do not recognize people as fixed assets on the balance sheet because human capital is context dependent; any calculation that is made by a firm may possibly have some meaning within the firm but is unlikely to be comparable with the calculations made by other firms so that benchmarking becomes pointless.

▌ The basis of the calculations may not be understood or accepted by investors if the results appear in external reports.

▌ The accountancy profession is doubtful about valuations of human assets because, unlike other forms of assets, eg physical assets, goodwill, people can leave the organization whenever they want.

However, in spite of these arguments it may be believed that there are powerful reasons as listed in Questionnaire 17 for at least attempting to evaluate human capital. There is a choice of methods as summarized in Table A.1.

Table A.1   Approaches to human capital evaluation

The Organizational Performance Model – Mercer Human Resource Consulting (Nalbantian *et al*, 2004)	The statistical tool 'Internal labour market analysis' used by Mercer draws on the running record of employee and labour market data to analyse the actual experience of employees rather than stated HR programmes and policies. Thus gaps can be identified between what is required in the workforce to support business goals and what is actually being delivered. It combines qualitative input from employee surveys and management interviews with hard, quantitative data from business operations, finance and HR.
The Human Capital Monitor (Mayo, 2001)	The Human Capital Monitor is used to identify the human value of the enterprise or 'human asset worth' which is equal to 'employment cost × individual asset multiplier'. The latter is a weighted average assessment of capability, potential to grow, personal performance (contribution) and alignment to the organization's values set in the context of the workforce environment (ie how leadership, culture, motivation and learning are driving success). The absolute figure is not important. What does matter is that the process of measurement leads you to consider whether human capital is sufficient, increasing or decreasing, and highlights issues to address.
The Newbury Index Rating (NIR) – Kearns (as reported by Dan Thomas in *Personnel Today*, 2005)	A rating is based on viewing the organization from a number of perspectives with the aim of producing a measure that clearly indicates how well the organization is managing to capitalize on the value of its people.
The Human Capital Report (Lees, 2004)	The result of the report is a number out of 100 that is an individual and group measure of human capital based on the mean performance scores from 360-degree feedback for individuals with the same competence profile.

Causal links between human capital and business performance

Defining the link between HR practices affecting the availability, engagement and development of human capital and business performance is the ultimate goal of HCM and the most difficult one to achieve. The aim is to be able to say on the basis of measurement: 'When we do this (an HR or people management practice), that (improved business results) will happen.' There is a choice of approach and questionnaire 18 provides a framework for evaluating the alternatives.

Questionnaire 18: Methods of calculating causal links between human capital and business performance

Method	Questions – answer 'yes' or 'no'			If 'yes' and we have the data and have or can acquire the skills, how are we going to develop the process?
	Is this approach of interest?	If 'yes':		
		Have we got the data?	Have we got the skills?	
The employee–customer–profit chain links employee satisfaction to customer satisfaction to profitability (cf Rucci *et al*, 1998)				
The Nationwide Building Society Genome II human capital investment model quantifies the impact that employee commitment has on customer satisfaction and business performance				
Business impact modelling (Mercer) predicts the outcome of specific people interventions and therefore anticipates the ROI from a particular programme (cf Mathewman, 2006)				
ROI – the net income generated from expenditure on an HR process, eg training (cf Kearns, 2005b)				

DEVELOP INTERNAL REPORTS

Purposeful measurement provides information that guides the formulation of strategy, assesses the contribution of people and people management practices to business results, and evaluates the effectiveness of line managers as people managers and the HR function to determine areas for improvement. The process of reporting the data and the inferences obtained from them is therefore a vital part of HCM. It is necessary to be clear about what data is required and for what purpose as considered in the section dealing with measurement in this toolkit. Questionnaire 19 provides a framework for analysing what should be included in reports.

Questionnaire 19: Content of internal reports

Information/conclusions to be included in internal reports	Required?	
	Yes	No
Quantitative and qualitative information – this could include data on the size and composition of the workforce, attraction and retention, absence, motivation, skills and competencies, learning and development activities, remuneration and fair employment practices, leadership and succession planning. It would also include analyses of trends and implications		
Information derived from employee opinion surveys with conclusions on the implications		
Measures of employee engagement and commitment compared with data on business performance and with an assessment of the links between them		
Analyses of the outcomes and implications of external benchmarking		
Identification of the key performance drivers in the organization with assessments of how HCM is contributing to adding value in each of these areas		
Review of the extent to which people management strategy, policies and practices are contributing to the achievement of business goals		
Calculations of the returns on investments in people management and development projects and evaluations of the effectiveness of the investments		
Informing line managers on their effectiveness as people managers		
Providing information on the efficiency and effectiveness of the HR function		
Drawing conclusions on the implications of the data for business strategy and future people management strategy, policy and practice		

DEVELOP EXTERNAL REPORTS

In considering what to do about external reporting of human capital information it is first necessary to consider the arguments for and against external reporting (Questionnaire 20). If the conclusion is favourable, the next step is to decide on the contents of the report and how the information should be assembled and presented (Questionnaire 21).

Questionnaire 20: *Arguments for and against external human capital reports*

Arguments for and against external capital reports		Agree	Partially agree	Disagree
Arguments for	Provide share owners and other stakeholders with information in the shape of metrics and qualitative assessments that will enable them to judge the extent to which the human capital arrangements of the business (leadership, talent management, skills availability, acquisition, retention, learning and development) enable the company to deliver its business strategy successfully			
	Demonstrate the organization's success in sourcing, managing and retaining the vital human capital it needs for business success			
	Provide information on the dynamics of the organization's human capital and how that is likely to affect performance in the future			
	Provide measurements (current and trends) on the value of the organization's human capital			
Arguments against	Human capital is not easily measured and there is a lack of standard, consistent metrics which could be applied to all companies or sectors			

Arguments for and against external capital reports	Agree	Partially agree	Disagree
Any information presented in an external report is likely to be so bland or riddled with assumptions as to be worthless and misleading			
Even if valid data can be identified it may be too confidential to be disclosed			
The possible benefits of the report may not justify the effort of collecting and analysing data			

Questionnaire 21: Content of external reports

Content of external reports	Definitely	Possibly	No
The profile of the workforce and its diversity			
Senior executive remuneration			
The quality of leadership and management strength			
How well labour costs have been managed over time			
Evidence of a coherent, robust people strategy that is mapped to the stated business strategy for the next three years			
Evidence that current people management practices (especially regarding acquisition, motivation and retention) are improving organizational and business performance			
Current and forecasted returns on people investment in the next three to five years			
The value of human capital assets and future investments, especially in major corporate decisions such as mergers and acquisitions			
Comparator listings in financial league tables – such as industry FTSE or analyst ratings			
Position in 'best company to work for' surveys			

HOW DO WE OPERATE HCM?

The steps required are:

▌ Analyse the level of competency in dealing with HCM possessed by HR staff (see below); brief senior management and line managers on the outputs of HCM and how they can be used (see below).

▌ Determine what measures will be required and make arrangements to collect and analyse the data (see Questionnaires 8–11 above).

▌ Determine what internal and external reports are required and make arrangements to prepare and issue them (see Questionnaires 18 and 20 above).

▌ Analyse and evaluate the outputs of HCM in order to guide decisions on how the human capital performance of the business should be presented, on the formulation and implementation of business and HR strategies and on the development of HR practices (Questionnaire 22).

Questionnaire 22: HR competence in HCM practice

It is necessary to analyse the skills required and available in HR to operate HCM using this questionnaire to identify any gaps so that remedial action can be taken.

HR competence	Required – yes or no	Fully available	Partially available	Not available
Understanding of the business – its strategies and key drivers				
Appreciation of how HR strategy can support the business strategy				
Knowledge of the data that can be used to measure organizational and individual performance and the performance of HR				
Understanding of what managers need in the way of data to help them to manage their people				
Knowledge of how to collect and analyse data				

HR competence	Required – yes or no	Fully available	Partially available	Not available
Knowledge of advanced statistical techniques such as correlation, regression analysis, factor analysis and multi-variant analysis				
Skills in preparing a business case supported by data and in persuading management to take action				
Skills in working as part of a management team				
Skills in working with the finance function				

Analysis of business strategy and business drivers

An analysis of the business strategy and drivers provides the basis for deciding where HR strategies can support the achievement of business goals and the information required to guide and review strategy. Table A.2 sets out typical strategy headings and drivers and the HR supporting activities and data that could be aligned to them. The framework it provides could be used in analysing your own strategies and drivers and the implications for HR strategy and human capital data requirements.

Table A.2 Analysis of business strategy and business drivers

	Content	HR supporting activities	Supporting data required
Business strategy	Growth – revenue/profit	HR planning	Workforce composition
		Talent management	Attrition rates
	Maximizing shareholder value	Skills development	Skills audit
	Growth through acquisitions/mergers	Targeted recruitment	Outcome of recruitment campaigns
		Retention policies	
	Growth in production/servicing facilities	Leadership development	Learning and development activity levels
	Product development		Outcome of leadership surveys
	Market development		
	Price/cost leadership		

	Content	HR supporting activities	Supporting data required
Business drivers	Innovation	Talent management	Balanced scorecard data
	Maximizing added value	Skills development	Added value ratios (eg added value per employee, added value per £ of employment cost)
	Productivity	Total reward management	
	Customer service	Performance management	
	Quality		
	Satisfying stakeholders – investors, shareholders, employees, elected representatives	Developing high-performance working	Productivity ratios (eg sales revenue per employee, units produced or serviced per employee)
		Enhancing motivation, engagement and commitment	
	Price/cost leadership	Leadership development	Outcomes of general employee opinion survey and other surveys covering engagement and commitment, leadership, reward management and performance management
			Analysis of competence level assessments
			Analysis of performance management assessments
			Analysis of customer surveys
			Analysis of outcomes of total quality programmes
			Return on investment from training activities
			Internal promotion rate
			Succession planning coverage

Analysis of HCM data requirements to support HR activities

The planning and day-to-day management of HCM needs to be related to the HR activities the HCM data is meant to inform and support. The main activities and their data requirements are set out in Table A.3. This framework could be used in analysing your own HR activities and their data requirements.

Table A.3 Applications of HCM

Activity	Definition	Data requirements
Talent management	The identification, attraction, retention, development and utilization of talent	Index of employee turnover
		Survival rates
		Half-life index
		Stability index
		Length of service analysis
		Cost of employee turnover
		Assessments of performance and potential obtained through performance management processes
		Analysis of data on who is available to succeed individuals in key jobs to identify gaps
Learning and development	The process by which a person acquires and develops new knowledge, skills, capabilities and attitudes and progresses from a present state of understanding and capability to a future state in which higher-level skills, knowledge and competencies are required	Evaluation of training Kirkpatrick's (1994) four steps
		Return on investment in training
		Trends in competency assessments
		Personal development plans completed as a percentage of employees
		Training hours per employee
		Percentage of managers taking part in formal development programmes

Activity	Definition	Data requirements
Knowledge management	The process of storing and sharing the wisdom, understanding and expertise accumulated in an organization about its processes, techniques and operations	Activity levels, eg the achievements of communities of interests in sharing knowledge and ensuring that it is put to good use
Performance management	A systematic process for improving organizational performance by developing the performance of individuals and teams	Percentage of employees taking part in formal performance reviews
		Distribution of performance ratings by category of staff and department
		Impact of performance management on business performance
		Performance management opinion survey
Reward management	The formulation and implementation of strategies and policies, the purposes of which are to reward people fairly, equitably and consistently in accordance with their value to the organization	Total payroll costs
		Compa-ratios (actual rates of pay as a percentage of policy rates)
		Total pay review increases for different categories of employees as a percentage of pay
		Average bonuses or contingent pay increases as a percentage of pay for different categories of employees
		Outcome of equal pay reviews (pay gaps)
Line manager development	Provision of information and advice to enable line managers to improve their performance	Leadership opinion survey 360-degree feedback

Activity	Definition	Data requirements
Enhancing job engagement and organizational commitment	Job engagement, takes place when people are committed to their work and motivated to achieve high levels of performance Organizational commitment is about identification with the goals and values of the organization, a desire to belong to the organization and a willingness to display effort on its behalf	Outcome of engagement and commitment survey

References

Accounting for People Task Force (2003) *Accounting for People*, DTI, London

Accounting Standards Board (ASB) (2003) *Statement on the Operating and Standards Review*, ASB, London

ASB (2004), *ASB PN 243, Press Release on the Way Forward on the OFR*, ASB, London

Armstrong, M and Baron, A (1998) *Performance Management: The new realities*, IPD, London

Armstrong, M and Baron, A (2004) *Managing Performance: Performance management in action*, CIPD, London

Armstrong, M and Brown D (2006) *Strategic Reward*, Kogan Page, London

Barney, J (1991) Firm resources and sustained competitive advantage, *Journal of Management*, 17, pp 99–120

Beatty, R W, Huselid, M A and Schneier, C E (2003) Scoring on the business scorecard, *Organizational Dynamics*, **32** (2), pp 107–21

Becker, G S (1975) *Human Capital: A theoretical and empirical analysis*, National Bureau of Economic Research, New York

Becker, B E, Huselid, M A, Pickus, P S and Spratt, M F (1997) HR as a source of shareholder value: research and recommendations, *Human Resource Management*, Spring, **36** (1), pp 39–47

Becker, B E, Huselid, M A and Ulrich, D (2001) *The HR Score Card: Linking people, strategy, and performance*, Harvard Business School Press, Boston, MA

Beer, M, Spector, B, Lawrence, P, Quinn Mills, D and Walton, R (1984) *Managing Human Assets*, The Free Press, New York

Blake, P (1998) The knowledge management expansion, *Information Today*, **15** (1), pp 12–13

Bontis, N (1996) There's a price on your head: managing intellectual capital strategically, *Business Quarterly*, Summer, pp 4–47

Bontis, N (1998) Intellectual capital: an exploratory study that develops measures and models, *Management Decision*, **36** (2), pp 63–76

Bontis, N, Dragonetti, N C, Jacobsen, K and Roos, G (1999) The knowledge toolbox: a review of the tools available to measure and manage intangible resources, *European Management Journal*, **17** (4), pp 391–402

Boudreau, J W (1988) Utility analysis, in *Human Resource Management: Evolving roles and responsibilities*, ed L Dyer, Bureau of National Affairs, Washington, DC

Boxall, P (1996) The strategic HRM debate and the resource-based view of the firm, *Human Resource Management Journal*, **6** (3), pp 59–75

Boxall, P (1999) Human resource strategy and competitive advantage: a longitudinal study of engineering consultancies, *Journal of Management Studies*, **36** (4), pp 443–63

Boxall, P and Purcell, J (2003) *Strategic Human Resource Management*, Palgrave Macmillan, Basingstoke

Brown, D (2006) Human interest, *People Management*, 23 March, p 7

Brown, D and Armstrong, M (1999) *Paying for Contribution: Real performance-related pay strategies*, Kogan Page, London

Cannon, T (2000) Knowledge entrepreneurs and the responsible corporation, in *Human Capital and Corporate Regulation*, ed Anthony Carey and Nigel Sleigh-Johnson, Institute of Chartered Accountants, London

CFO Research Services (2003) *Human Capital Management: The CFO's perspective*, CFO Publishing, Boston, MA

Chatzkel, J L (2004) Human capital: the rules of engagement are changing, *Lifelong Learning in Europe*, **9** (3), pp 139–145

Chartered Institute of Personnel and Development (CIPD) (2003) *Human Capital: External reporting framework*, CIPD, London

CIPD (2004) *Human Capital Reporting: An internal perspective*, CIPD, London

CIPD (2006a) *Human Capital Evaluation: Getting Started*, CIPD, London.

CIPD (2006b) *Human Capital Evaluation: Evolving the Data*, CIPD, London.

Coleman, J S (1990) *Foundations of Social Theory*, University of Harvard Press, Cambridge, MA

Daft, R L and Weick, K E (1984) Towards a model of organisations as interpretation systems, *Academy of Management Review*, 9, pp 284–95

Davenport, T O (1999) *Human Capital*, Jossey Bass, San Francisco

Davenport, T H and Prusak, L (1998) *Working Knowledge: How organizations manage what they know*, Harvard Business School Press, Boston, MA

deLong, T and Vijayaraghavan, V (2003) Let's hear it for B players, *Harvard Business Review*, June, pp 96–102

Department of Trade and Industry (DTI) (2004) *The Operating and Financial Review, Practical guidance for directors*, Operating and Financial Review Working Group on Materiality, DTI, London

Donkin, R (2005) *Human Capital Management: A management report*, Croner, London

Dyer, L and Holder, G W (1998) Strategic human resource management and planning, in *Human Resource Management: Evolving roles and responsibilities*, ed L Dyer, Bureau of National Affairs, Washington DC

Edvinson, L and Malone, M S (1997) *Intellectual Capital: Realizing your company's true value by finding its hidden brainpower*, Harper Business, New York

Ehrenberg, R G and Smith, R S (1997) *Modern Labor Economics*, 6th edn, HarperCollins, New York

Elliott, R F (1991) *Labor Economics*, McGraw-Hill, Maidenhead

Fitz-enj, J (2000) *The ROI of Human Capital*, American Management Association, New York

Fombrun, C J, Tichy, N M, and Devanna, M A (1984) *Strategic Human Resource Management*, New York, Wiley

Galbraith, J R (1973) *Organizational Design*, Addison-Wesley, Reading, MA

Ghoshal, S and Bartlett, C A (1993) Changing the role of top management: beyond structure to process, *Harvard Business Review*, January–February, pp 86–96

Gillen, S (2006), It's not just figures that give investors answers, *Professional Investor*, March, pp 16–20

Grant, R M (1991) The resource-based theory of competitive advantage: implications for strategy formulation, *California Management Review*, **33** (3), pp 114–35

Guest, D E (1987) Human resource management and industrial relations, *Journal of Management Studies*, **14** (5), pp 503–21

Guest, D E and Hoque, K (1994) Yes, personnel management does make the difference, *Personnel Management*, November, pp 40–44

Hamel, G and Prahalad, C K (1989) Strategic intent, *Harvard Business Review*, May–June, pp 63–76

Hartley, V and Robey, D (2005) *Reporting on Human Capital Management*, IIES, Brighton

Hendry, C and Pettigrew, A (1986) The practice of strategic human resource management, *Personnel Review*, 15, pp 2–8

Hermanson, R (1964) *Accounting for Human Assets*, Bureau of Business and Economic Research, Michigan State University, Occasional Paper, November

Higgins, N J (2005) Head to head, *Personnel Today*, 22 November, p 15

Huselid, M A, Jackson, S E, Schuler, R S (1997) Technical and strategic human resource management effectiveness as determinants of firm performance, *Academy of Management Journal*, **40** (1) pp 171–88

Hutchinson, S and Purcell, J (2003) *Bringing Policies to Life: The vital role of front line managers in people management*, CIPD, London

IDS (2004) Searching for the magic bullet, *HR Study 783*, October pp 2–6

IRS (2004) Human capital reporting: proving the value of people, *IRS Employment Review 802*, 18 June, pp 9–15

IRS (2005a) Building human capital investment at Nationwide, *IRS Employment Review 819*, 11 March, pp 15–17

IRS (2005b) The tip of the iceberg: human capital reporting, *IRS Employment Review 837*, 16 December, pp 8–14

Kaplan, R S and Norton, D P (1992) The balanced scorecard – measures that drive performance, *Harvard Business Review*, January–February, pp 71–79

Kaplan, R S and Norton, D P (1996) *The Balanced Scorecard*, Harvard Business School Press, Boston, MA

Kearns, P (2005a) *Human Capital Management*, Reed Business Information, Sutton, Surrey

Kearns, P (2005b) *Evaluating the ROI From Learning*, CIPD, London

Kearns, P (2006) What do we mean by human capital management? In *What's the Future for Human Capital?*, CIPD, London

Kearns, P and Miller, T (1997) Measuring the impact of training and development on the bottom line, *FT Management Briefings*, Pitman, London

Kinnie, N, Swart, J, Morris, S, Snell, S and Kang, S-C (2006) *Managing People and Knowledge in Professional Service Firms*, CIPD, London

Kirkpatrick, D L (1994) *Evaluating Training Programs*, Berret-Koehler, San Francisco

Lawler, E E (2003) Current performance management practices, *WorldatWork Journal*, **12** (2), pp 21–30

Leadbeater, C (2000) *New Measures for the New Economy*, Centre for Business Performance, London

Lees, H (2004) Measuring human capital, *Human Resources (New Zealand)*, **9** (5) pp 14–17

Legge, K (1998) The morality of HRM, in *Experiencing Human Resource Management*, ed C Mabey, D Skinner and T Clark, Sage, London

Lepak, D P and Snell, S A (1999) The human resource architecture: toward a theory of human capital allocation and development, *Academy of Management Review*, **24** (1), pp 31–48

Lewin, K (1947) Frontiers in group dynamics, *Human Relations*, **1** (1), pp 5–42

Likert, R (1967) *The Human Organization*, McGraw-Hill, New York

Likierman, A (2005) How to measure the performance of HRM, *People Management*, 11 August, pp 44–45

Longbotham, D (2005) Head to head, *Personnel Today*, 22 November

Manocha, R (2005) Grand totals, *People Management*, 7 April, pp 27–31

Mathewman, J (2006) Focus on measurement, in *What's the Future for Human Capital?*, CIPD, London

Mayo, A (1999) Making human capital meaningful, *Knowledge Management Review*, January–February, pp 26–29

Mayo, A (2001) *The Human Value of the Enterprise: Valuing people as assets*, Nicholas Brealey, London

Mayo, A (2004) Making it all add up, *Personnel Today*, 24 February, pp 23–24

Mayo, A (2006) Measuring and reporting – the fundamental requirement for data, in *What's the Future for Human Capital?*, CIPD, London

Mercer Human Resource Consulting, (2004) *Human capital and business performance: Measuring the links*, New York, Mercer Human Resource Consulting

McDonald, D and Smith, A (1991) A proven connection: performance management and business results, *Compensation & Benefits Review*, January–February, pp 59–64

Murlis, H (2005) Diverse engagement factors, e-*reward/CIPD Reward Symposium*, (unpublished)

Nalbantian, R, Guzzo, R A, Kieffer, D and Doherty, J (2004), *Play to Your Strengths: Managing your internal labour markets for lasting competitive advantage*, McGraw-Hill, New York

Neely, A (1998) *Measuring Business Performance*, Economist/Profile Books, London

Operating and Financial Review Working Group on Materiality (2004), *The Operating and Financial Review, Practical guidance for directors*, DTI, London

Oracle (2005) *Human Capital Management*, People Management, London

Organization for Economic Co-operation and Development (OECD) (1998) *Human Capital Investment: An International Comparison*, OECD, Paris

Outram, R (1998) Mental arithmetic, *Human Resources*, October, pp 77–79

Penna Consulting (2003) *Taking Measures*, Penna Consulting, London

Penrose, E (1959) *The Theory of the Growth of the Firm*, Blackwell, Oxford

People Management (2006) Firms urged to report on human capital, 27 July, p 12

Personnel Today (2004) HCM must be kept simple if HR wants to engage staff, 7 December, p 3

Pickard, J (2005) Part not partner, *People Management*, 27 October, pp 48–50

Purcell, J, Kinnie, K, Hutchinson, Rayton, B and Swart, J (2003) *People and Performance: How people management impacts on organisational performance*, CIPD, London

Putnam, R (1996) Who killed civic America?, *Prospect*, March, pp 66–72

Rucci, A J, Kirn, S P and Quinn, R T (1998) The employee-customer-profit chain at Sears, *Harvard Business Review*, January–February, pp 82–97

Sackmann, S, Flamholz, E and Bullen, M (1989), Human asset accounting, *Journal of Accounting Literature*, 5, pp 235–64

Saratoga (2005) *Key Trends in Human Capital: A global perspective*, PricewaterhouseCoopers, London

Scarborough, H and Elias, J (2002) *Evaluating Human Capital*, CIPD, London

Scarborough, H, Swan, J and Preston, J (1999) *Knowledge Management: A literature review*, IPD, London

Schein, E H (1969) *Process Consultation: Its role in organizational development*, Addison-Wesley, Reading, MA

Schuller, T (2000) Social and human capital; the search for appropriate technomethodology, *Policy Studies*, **21** (1), pp 25–35

Schultz, T W (1961) Investment in human capital, *American Economic Review*, 51, March, pp 1–17

Schultz, T W (1981) *Investing in People: The economics of population quality*, University of California, CA

Scott-Jackson, W, Cook, P and Tajer, R (July 2006) *Measures of workforce capability for future performance*, Chartered Management Institute, London

Smethurst, S (2005) The long and winding road, *People Management*, 28 July, pp 25–29

Smilansky, J (2005) *The Systematic Management of Executive Talent*, Hydrogen, London

Smith, A (1776) *The Wealth of Nations*, Clarendon, Oxford

Suff, R (2005) Building human capital investment at Nationwide, *IRS Employment Review 819*, 11 March, pp 15–17

Syrett, M (2006) Four reflections on developing a human capital measurement capability, *What's the Future for Human Capital?*, CIPD, London

Tan, J (2000) Knowledge management – just more buzzwords? *British Journal of Administrative Management*, March–April, pp 10–11

Thomas, D (2005) Where would you rate on new HCM league table?, *Personnel Today*, 7 June, p 6

Thompson, P (2002) *Total Reward*, CIPD, London

Tsui, A S and Gomez-Mejia, L R (1988) Evaluating human resource effectiveness, in *Human Resource Management: Evolving roles and responsibilities*, ed L Dyer, Bureau of National Affairs, Washington, DC

Tyson, S and Witcher, M (1994) Getting in gear: post-recession HR management, *Personnel Management*, August, pp 20–23

Ulrich, D (1998) A new mandate for human resources, *Harvard Business Review*, January–February, pp 124–34

Ulrich, D and Brockbank, W (2005a) *The HR Value Proposition*, Harvard Press, Cambridge, MA

Ulrich, D and Brockbank, W (2005b) Role call, *People Management*, 16 June, pp 24–28

Ulrich, D and Lake, D (1991) Organizational capability: creating competitive advantage, *Academy of Management Executive*, **7** (1), pp 77–92

Walker, J W (1992) *Human Resource Strategy*, McGraw-Hill, New York

Walters, M (2006) What is the role of HR process? *What's the Future for Human Capital?*, CIPD, London

Watkins, K and Marsick, V (1993) *Sculpting the Learning Organization,* Falmer Press, London

Watson Wyatt Worldwide, (2002) *Human Capital Index®: Human capital as a lead indicator of shareholder value,* Watson Wyatt Worldwide, Washington, DC

World Bank (2000) website: worldbank.org

Youndt, M A (2000) Human resource considerations and value creation: the mediating role of intellectual capital, paper delivered at National Conference of US Academy of Management, Toronto, August

Subject index

Names index